Is There Absolute Truth?

IS THERE ABSOLUTE TRUTH?

Why It Doesn't Matter

What **YOU** *Believe*

If It's Not True

Stephen McAndrew

Deep River Books
Sisters, Oregon
http://www.deepriverbooks.com

13-digit ISBN: 9781935265979
10-digit ISBN: 1935265970

Library of Congress: 2012930159

Printed in the USA

Cover design by Joe Bailen, Contajus Designs

DEDICATION

To Michelle,
my unwavering supporter; and
Hannah, John, and Sarah: my inspiration.

TABLE OF CONTENTS

Chapter 1   Introduction 9

Chapter 2   Footnotes to Plato 15

Chapter 3   The Tyranny of Freedom from Absolute Truth 25

Chapter 4   Can We Believe in Universal Human Rights &
             Moral Relativism Simultaneously? 33

Chapter 5   The Contingency Contradiction 43

Chapter 6   Re-Imagining Reality 49

Chapter 7   What Might a Source of the Human Rights
             Urge Look Like? 59

Chapter 8   On Hedonism 67

Chapter 9   This is My Truth - A la Carte Belief 71

Chapter 10   Some Thoughts on Art 77

Chapter 11   Final Thoughts 83

             Notes 87

Chapter One

Introduction

"The unexamined life is not worth living."

—Socrates[1]

This book is not in a strict sense a technical philosophical work. It is more of an extended essay that is philosophical in nature. My goal is to challenge suppositions often considered unassailable. But, is this not the essence of philosophical activity: to logically examine even the most comfortable of our belief structures and leave standing only those that survive the disciplined assault of reason?

As you continue to read, you may think I am making bold claims, and indeed I am. However, through the course of this book, I will explain why I hold these positions. My goal is to do so in a reasoned manner that will not alienate those who initially disagree with my thesis. I do not wish to add to the many shrill voices viciously assailing each other on moral issues in our society today.

I hope you will approach this book with an open mind and hear me through. My arguments, which are hardly novel,[2] are set forth in the following pages in as clear and concise a manner as my powers of argument permit. So, for my part, I will not be insulted if, after completing this book, you have not been convinced absolute truth does exist.

As a starting point, imagine someone at a political rally protesting torture, armed with placards, denouncing the motives and moral well-being of those the protester holds responsible for various atrocities. Ask the protester why he or she is driven to speak out and the protester replies, "Torture is wrong." Then ask this same person how he or she knows torture is wrong. He or she will probably look at you as if you are crazy.

Everyone knows certain things are right and certain things are wrong. Isn't that just the way it is?

The hypothetical protester described is a moral absolutist. That is to say, he or she holds that certain moral truths are fixed and do not vary according to time or place. Throughout this book I describe such objective truths as absolute truths. As I will draw out through the course of this book, if the protester was to claim to be a moral relativist, his or her claim that torture is wrong would be meaningless.

Conversely, pose the following question to another person on the street: are there absolute right answers to moral questions, like euthanasia or abortion? If the person questioned holds to a version of moral relativism, he or she will most likely reply that these issues are not black and white, and cannot be satisfied by dogmatic answers.

Moral relativism is the theory that moral truth is not absolute because it changes over time and varies according to many factors including the society we find ourselves living in. The prevailing wisdom of post-modern society is that truth, and in particular, moral truth, is relative. Yet, this adherence to moral relativism runs counter to another strong current of post-modern society—the emergence of universal human rights laws that are held to apply to all people, in all societies.

The central aim of this thesis is to examine the tension between moral relativism and what I will refer to as *the human rights urge*, and to explore where the resolution of this conflict brings us.

THIS IS MY TRUTH

The extent of the current acceptance of the relativity of truth is evidenced by the proliferation of subjective idiosyncratic beliefs. In the United States, National Public Radio (NPR) recently broadcasted a series of monologues delivered by people from all walks of life called *This I Believe*.[3] During each of the short broadcasts, the commentators (some of whom were well-known, but most of whom were not) expressed beliefs they personally held to be true.

A striking element of these belief statements was the subjective nature of the beliefs expressed. The proponents were not trying to convince others to share their beliefs. The tone was not preachy, but pragmatic: "This is my truth."

Many of the participants expressed beliefs that worked for them. Many of them arrived at their beliefs out of personal experience. The proponents made no attempt to evaluate whether or not their beliefs were true. If the belief worked for its holder that was good enough.

In addition, a popular coffee shop chain dispenses morsels of wisdom from time-to-time with each cup of coffee. Various beliefs are printed on disposable beverage containers—a brief sentence or two expressed by the holder of the belief. We can order a cup of coffee in hundreds of different ways to create our own individual beverage. Likewise, we like to form our *own* unique beliefs.

These examples demonstrate the importance we place upon believing in something, be it world peace, Jesus, Buddha, or change. They also highlight the high value society places on personal belief, however peculiar.

The tendency to subjective belief is reinforced by the increasing balkanization of culture. Increasingly, people interact with other people who tend to hold the same views on things. There are magazines, web sites, and radio and television stations catering to specific social and political beliefs. A person can spend the majority of his or her time surrounded by ideas and beliefs that resonate with them and avoid arguments that might challenge their worldview.

Moreover, we are fed ideas in small sound bites that are really just the conclusions of particular beliefs. We do not examine what underpins these sound bites. If the sound bites are presented by a source we are accustomed to accepting as true, there is a danger we will assimilate the conclusion without knowing, or caring, whether it is based on solid arguments and assumptions.

So, the idea that one person's moral viewpoint is no more correct than another person's is widely subscribed to. Often the motivation behind moral relativism is tolerance—not to be perceived to impose your personal beliefs on others. The underlying assumption is that convictions and beliefs are a fiercely personal matter. There is no question that whether truth is relative or absolute, our deepest convictions remain individual at their core.

But, if truth is absolute and not relative, subjective beliefs are of little value unless they somehow describe something about ultimate reality. So, if truth is absolute, we should examine all subjective truths presented to us in an effort to determine which of the ideas presented (if any) are true. However, clearly individual beliefs, whether presented in a radio commentary or on the side of a disposable coffee cup, are valued in our society for being individual, not for being absolutely true.

Relatively Inconsistent

The examples above highlight the fact that post-modern culture holds that whatever you believe is okay because there are no absolute truths. But, we do not consistently apply moral relativism. In many situations (e.g., condemning torture), we act like we are surrounded by absolute truths. This is because we do not draw out the theory of moral relativism to its logical conclusion.

As will be explained in more detail, if all truth is relative, we cannot morally condemn the actions or attitudes of others because they diverge from our moral concepts and rules. According to a consistent application of moral relativism, a person's actions should be judged within the framework of his or her moral belief system, not ours.

English philosopher Thomas Hobbes famously wrote that life in an unordered society would be "nasty, brutish and short."[4] The same would be true for life in a society without absolute moral standards. In a world with no method for distinguishing between right and wrong, no one could be sure that things he or she believes should be morally prohibited are in fact wrong. In such a world, I might condemn the acts of a murderer as barbaric, but if there is no reliable framework to aid me in classifying the murderer's actions as wrong or evil, I cannot be sure that my moral judgment is correct. Likewise I cannot commend the actions of a charity worker who gives up a lucrative career to help those in need. Even a genocidal maniac could not be considered evil.

In the first part of this book, I argue that we do not live in a world without absolutes. I trace the philosophical underpinnings of moral relativism, particularly the theory that truth is dependent upon indoctrination by society. Then I point out (as some honest moral relativists have), that those who argue all truth is relative must accept the fact they cannot condemn others for moral beliefs divergent from their own. The end point of moral relativism is despair. One cannot be a moral relativist and scream against genocide. Further, in a world without absolute truth, concepts like freedom and equality are not set in stone and so not guaranteed to endure.

Consequently, a world without absolute truth also makes a mockery of the philosophical basis for modern international human rights law. One cannot condemn war criminals or punish them for violating the norms of international human rights law if moral relativism is correct. I will argue that this is not a world many of us are willing to accept or live in.

I hope most people shown the logical conclusion of the post-modern wisdom of relativism will reject it in favor of absolute truth and absolute moral standards. We may not all agree on which truths are absolute, but we can conclude that at least some ideas—freedom and justice—are universal to every human and should not be abridged. If proof is needed, some of our most cherished texts such as the Universal Declaration of Human Rights evidence our acceptance of universal truths.

The second part of this book argues that if there are absolute truths, there are right and wrong answers concerning moral questions and the ultimate nature of reality. If we accept the existence of absolute truths, we should also examine whether our personal beliefs match ultimate reality. Why? Because if absolute truths exist, and we can be mistaken about truth, personal beliefs are inadequate if they do not correspond (or make a decent effort to correspond) to the ultimate truths of our existence.

In addition, because the existence of absolute truth raises the stakes, we should not blindly accept what we are told. We must make energetic strides to challenge our ideas and vigorously examine the underpinnings of our beliefs to match our beliefs onto the ultimate furniture *of the universe*, what really exists, or at least to examine whether such a project is feasible.

If, like me, you conclude there are absolute moral truths out there to be discovered, you must then question the source of these absolutes. If these moral standards are eternal and immutable, they cannot be based on society and its changing mores. Neither can they be subjective individually-held beliefs that change with our whims. They must exist outside of both our society and ourselves.

Much of Western philosophy has been concerned with leaving metaphysics behind and grounding philosophy on firmer ground—making it more scientific and reasonable. However, I contend that reason does not necessarily lead to the abandonment of metaphysics and other so-called superstitions such as the belief in an immutable eternal God as a source for moral truth.

In fact, I believe that reason will ultimately bring us to realization that certain truths cannot be neatly verified in a scientific or philosophical manner. The most important truths are only discoverable through contemplation of truths that exist independently of the everyday.

So finally, I argue that the inescapable conclusion of reason is that absolute truth does exist. However, to answer the ultimate questions about the nature of reality and moral truth, we must look beyond philosophy and science because absolute truth transcends these realms.

In summary, if the existence of absolute ideas is granted, we cannot hide our heads in the sand and think that generating our own personal beliefs in a vacuum will suffice. To do so would be to live an unexamined and inauthentic life, because if we accept that absolute truth exists, it doesn't matter what we believe—if it's not true.

CHAPTER TWO

FOOTNOTES TO PLATO

"The safest general characterization of the European philosophical tradition is that it consists of a series of footnotes to Plato."

—ALFRED NORTH WHITEHEAD[1]

The very modern (or should I say post-modern) idea that there are no absolute moral truths and so no absolute moral standards can be traced in Western philosophy from Ancient Greece to the late twentieth century. It has been said Western philosophy consisted of footnotes to Plato.[2] However, a paradigm shift in the twentieth century led many to recognize that this was no longer the case.

The Austrian philosopher, Ludwig Wittgenstein, was the inspiration of much of this paradigm shift. This chapter traces the shift from the paradigm of Plato to the paradigm of Wittgenstein.

Plato set in place a framework that posited the existence of immutable absolute truths outside of our physical world in his theory of the Forms. In order to put philosophy on a more empirical scientific footing, later thinkers attempted to free philosophy from having to accept the existence of absolute metaphysical truths. However, their solutions ended up creating more problems such as whether one could prove the existence of the external world outside of one's mind or the existence of minds other than one's own.

Wittgenstein proposed solving the question of where ideas come from by theorizing that all of our ideas come from the community into which we are born and raised. However, a consequence of the theory that ideas are community-based is that there can be no absolute moral truths and therefore no absolute moral standards.

Ancient Dogma?

The ancient Greek philosopher Plato held that all concepts and ideas that exist in our world are based on Forms of these objects or ideas that exist outside of space and time. He maintained the Forms are unchangeable and eternal and that the concepts and ideas encountered in the everyday world are merely imperfect reflections of the Forms.

Plato claimed that we had knowledge of the Forms before we were born. He further asserted that we are born with imperfect intuitive knowledge of the Forms and this intuitive knowledge helps us to recognize concepts and ideas we encounter in our everyday world. For example, I can know what justice is because I am somehow aware of the Form of justice.

In *Republic*, Plato provides the famous cave allegory to explain the theory of the Forms.[3] He wrote that living in our world is like living in a cave. We are forced to sit inside the cave with our backs to the entrance of the cave looking at a cave wall. There is a fire at our backs illuminating the cave, and as people pass the entrance of the cave, shadows of these people and the objects they hold are seen on the cave wall in front of us.

We think the shadows made on the cave wall by the outside objects are the real objects themselves. Plato gave the cave allegory to describe life in our world. He asserted that the ideas and objects we experience are not the real ideas or objects in themselves, but only shadows of the Forms that exist outside of space and time. We think something is beautiful because the object in some way relates to the Form of beauty. Similarly, we know what love is only because it relates to the Form of love.

Plato's theory of the Forms is a *correspondence theory* of *truth*.[4] In other words, his theory maintains that the words we use have objective meanings that can be discovered. This can be contrasted with a *coherence theory* of truth, which contends that our words have meaning if they make sense when placed together with other words that we use.[5] The obvious question then is: where do the Forms exist?

Plato believed, as many religions do, in an ultimate reality separate from our everyday world, of which we have some partial intuitive or innate knowledge. He believed that before we are born we have access to the Forms, and as we go through life, we reacquaint ourselves with them. According to this worldview, our ideas and concepts have absolute meanings, which can be discovered if we can access the higher world. Plato contended that the task of the philosopher is to discover the true nature of the Forms.

Plato's theory of the Forms posits absolute unchanging truths and therefore absolute moral standards. If we want to know what is *good*, we must try to discover the Form of *good* and determine if a proposed action lines up with *good*.

The theory of the Forms fits with traditional religious beliefs in a metaphysical or spiritual realm. Many religious belief systems maintain there are absolute metaphysical truths revealed to the faithful by way of supernatural revelation. Further, believers know the difference between right and wrong because these absolute truths are somehow divinely hardwired into human consciousness.

Many philosophers became uncomfortable with Plato's theory of the Forms because it logically led to a belief in a reality outside of our everyday physical world, which was increasingly thought to be at odds with the progress of scientific discovery. Science could not and cannot prove or disprove the existence of a metaphysical realm where the Forms exist. Consequently, philosophers sought to establish the origins of human knowledge on more secure, scientifically verifiable grounds.

A MORE SCIENTIFIC APPROACH

A group of philosophers in the seventeenth and eighteenth centuries, who became known as Empiricists, attempted to use objective scientific methods to discover ultimate truths about reality. They contended that only sensory perception could be trusted to give us a true picture of reality. In their quest to put philosophy on firmer ground in accordance with the emergence of modern science, they rejected metaphysical doctrines like Plato's Forms. However, the move to discover the origins of human knowledge using sense perception as the foundation led down a serious philosophical cul-de-sac that dragged the whole discipline of philosophy into disrepute.

David Hume, the Scottish philosopher and historian, was one of the best-known Empiricist philosophers. Like other Empiricist philosophers, he believed the only reliable information we can have about the world around us comes through our senses (*i.e., sight, sound, touch, smell, and taste*).

Hume argued we form ideas about the world from the raw data we receive from our senses. External objects we perceive are, in fact, mental representations we construct in our minds from sense data.

So, for example, when we perceive a table we receive certain information through our senses, and from this sense data we construct the picture of a table in our mind. Hume contended that even properties of the table such as firmness, temperature, color, and extension are not contained in the table, but are impressions in our mind.

However, because the Empiricists believed only sense data and not the representations we construct from sense data in our minds could be relied upon, a serious problem arose. Since we do not directly perceive the external objects in themselves, but only receive sense data that we turn into representations of external objects in our minds, we cannot be sure external objects exist independently of our minds.

Indeed, we know our senses can sometimes be mistaken. For example, we may see a mirage on a hot clear day. So, how can we be sure our senses are giving us a correct picture of the external world, or that the representations we construct from sense data are accurate reflections of the world around us? Therefore, if we leave the room where the table is, and its image is no longer in our minds, we cannot be sure it remains in existence.

Further, if the only reliable information we have of the world comes through our senses and is interpreted in our minds, and we cannot know that external objects exist outside of our minds, we cannot be sure that other minds exist. We can infer other people have minds like we do, but a strict Empiricist interpretation of the world only provides us with certainty regarding the inside of our own heads and not the heads of our neighbors.

In *Enquiries Concerning Human Understanding and Concerning the Principles of Morals*, Hume explained the problem:

> ...*philosophy which teaches us, that nothing can ever be present to the mind but an image or perception, and that the senses are the only inlets, through which these images are conveyed, without being able to produce any immediate intercourse between the mind and the object. The table, which we see, seems to diminish, as we remove farther from it: but the real table, which exists independent of us, suffers no alteration: it was, therefore, nothing but an image, which was present to the mind.*[6]

The end result of Empiricism was skepticism about the existence of the external world and other minds. German philosopher Immanuel Kant called this *the scandal of philosophy*,[7] and it frustrated even the Empiricists.

Hume recognized that this problem became ridiculous as he went about his daily life. He wrote:

> *Most fortunately it happens, that since reason is incapable of dispelling these clouds, [of skeptical doubt] nature herself suffices to that purpose, and cures me of this philosophical melancholy and delirium...I dine, I play a game of back-gammon, I converse, and am merry with friends; and when after three or four hours amusement, I wou'd return to these speculations, they appear so cold, and so strain's and ridiculous, that I cannot find in my heart to enter into them any further.*[8]

LOGICAL POSITIVISM

Building on the Empiricist tradition that only truths that can be verified in an empirical manner are meaningful was an early twentieth century philosophical movement known as *logical positivism*. The logical positivists took their inspiration from a group of Austrian thinkers labeled the *Vienna Circle*. The early work of Ludwig Wittgenstein, encapsulated in his book *Tractatus Logico-Philosophicus*, was a major influence on this group.

Logical positivism entailed the rejection as meaningless of any statements whose truthfulness or falsity could not be determined by strictly empirical methods.[9] So, scientific statements such as "water freezes at a certain temperature" were meaningful because the truth of this statement can be evaluated by scientific experimentation. One will cool water to the desired temperature, and either it will freeze or it will not. So in the eyes of the logical positivists this was a meaningful statement.

On the contrary, a statement such as "torture is morally wrong" was considered meaningless by the logical positivists. The truth or falsity of this statement could not be empirically verified. Similarly, the statement "Venus de Milo is a beautiful work of art" was meaningless in the eyes of the logical positivists because it too was incapable of empirical verification. Of course, logical positivism was also fatal to belief in the divine, as the existence or non-existence of God cannot be empirically verified.

Logical positivism was appealing because it provided a clean and crisp method of evaluating whether a proposition was true or false, but it abandoned vast swathes of the human experience as meaningless rubbish.

The Post-Modern Theory of Relativity

Following in the wake of logical positivism, the next wave of twentieth century philosophers tried to move away from an untenable philosophical position that led to doubts about the existence of the external world, without the radical rejection of propositions that cannot be empirically verified advanced by the logical positivists.

The Empiricists rejected a model of the world requiring *a priori* or intuitive knowledge of absolute truths existing on a metaphysical plane, such as Plato's theory of the Forms, but ended up not sure that anything existed. The logical positivists then rejected metaphysics entirely. For them, questions about whether we could be sure of the existence of the external world or other minds were non-questions.

After the logical positivists, a philosophical movement gathered steam that insisted on restarting the philosophical project by examining reality as we find it. Members of this movement contended that the problems of philosophy arose because philosophers had taken a subject-object view of the world.

Traditional philosophers like Plato viewed the philosopher as an objective onlooker examining reality as a scientist looking at a specimen through a microscope. However, twentieth century philosophers like Ludwig Wittgenstein and Martin Heidegger rejected this paradigm. Wittgenstein and Heidegger[10] insisted that the philosopher was situated in the everyday physical world and could not separate him or herself from the world to examine it coldly. This, they believed, would bring an end to the philosophical project and reveal the previously intractable skeptical problems of philosophy to be non-problems.

We started this chapter with a reference to Western philosophy being viewed as a series of footnotes to Plato until Ludwig Wittgenstein appeared on the philosophical scene. In his earlier career, Wittgenstein adhered to a correspondence theory of truth and did believe in absolute truths, but he did not think we could know these truths because they were beyond the limits of human understanding.[11]

But, it is Wittgenstein's later work that we will concern ourselves with for the remainder of this chapter. Wittgenstein in his later work developed a community-based theory to explain reality. He considered this theory to have solved the *scandal of philosophy* by ending the philosophical project to discover an absolute reality outside of our physical world.

He argued it was futile to search for objective and absolute meanings for our everyday ideas or to try to transcend our everyday existence to arrive at a greater reality in which absolute truths exist. He held that we received our ideas from the communities into which we were born.

Our communities inducted us into language-games that taught us about our world. These community ideas were not *a priori* intuitions of absolute truth; they were ideas and concepts developed by a society over time.

In *Philosophical Investigations*, Wittgenstein condemned the urge to try to look beneath or behind the everyday world in which we find ourselves. He contended that because philosophers kept trying to uncover a great system linking everything together, philosophy had ended up in such a muddle that it could not prove the existence of the external world.

For him, community-indoctrinated ideas were all there was, and so trying to discover some great system behind it all of course tied philosophers up in knots. Like David Hume, Wittgenstein was fed up with philosophical problems such as trying to prove the existence of the external world and other minds.

He wrote:

> So in the end, when one is doing philosophy, one gets to the point where one would like just to emit an inarticulate sound.[12]

Wittgenstein maintained philosophical confusion about the existence of the external world and other minds stemmed from a mistaken view of language. Instead of using language to express thoughts we already have in our minds, he contended it is only by learning language that we can have any thoughts at all.

Wittgenstein argued that language consisted of a series of language-games we are trained to play as we learn language. He held there were a multitude of language-games, from pointing at an object and giving it a name, to following orders. Language-games were part of human custom, or what it was like to live in society and be human, what he called forms of life.[13]

In our everyday lives we play language-games, and society could not function if we did not share an understanding of these language-games. For example, we can know when someone else is in pain because we too have been inducted into the language-game of pain.[14]

Therefore, if I see someone hopping on one foot and holding his other foot in his hand after dropping a hammer, I know this person is in pain. Pain is not therefore something private to me but a concept that I, and others socialized into the language-game of pain, can understand.

The forms of life into which we are trained are the same for everyone in a particular society. We are gradually trained in language-games and so initiated into forms of life by older members of our society. We start with simple language-games and move to increasingly complicated language-games as our acquisition of language progresses. Older members of our society reward us when we play a language-game correctly and admonish us when we fail to do so.

For instance, if a young child falls and scrapes her knee, she is rewarded by a hug or other consoling words or gestures if she cries out in pain. She has correctly played the language-game of being in pain. On the other hand, if she does not react to her misadventure and cry out, she will not be rewarded with consoling gestures and may even be treated coldly.

Wittgenstein claimed it made no sense for anyone to have a private language in his or her own mind. He asserted language was a set of public rules and so it would not work if we had our own private concepts of *pain* or *red* because we would not be able to communicate with other people.[15]

Since Wittgenstein asserted language was public and not private in nature, the problem of whether other minds existed also disappeared. His theory that language was public pre-supposed everyone has a mind so that he or she can understand and participate in language.

The view that our ideas are values based on the society into which we are born has its philosophical underpinnings in the philosophical work of Wittgenstein and other philosophers who followed in his wake. This view logically compels the adoption of a relative system of moral belief.

If moral ideas and values are taught to us by our culture as we grow up and develop language, our moral values will be different depending on the society into which we are born. Therefore, if one society or group condemns the moral beliefs of another society or group, they will be merely stating, "Those are not the moral values of our society." They cannot conclude their values are better.

In the following chapter, the consequences of a world without absolute moral truths, entailed by Wittgenstein's community-based theory of truth, will be sketched out in more detail.

CHAPTER THREE

THE TYRANNY OF FREEDOM FROM ABSOLUTE TRUTH

*"If you want a picture of the future, imagine a boot stamping
on a human face—forever."*

—GEORGE ORWELL[1]

Contending that our ideas and, therefore, our moral standards are derived from community indoctrination gets rid of the problem of having to believe, like Plato, in a metaphysical world where absolute truths reside. It also avoids the Empiricist philosophers' difficulties proving the existence of the external world and other minds.

However, if we are to accept that our ideas, including our moral standards, are community-based, we have to stomach the consequences that follow if no idea is universal or absolutely true.

WHEN IN ROME, DO AS THE ROMANS DO

Jean-Paul Sartre, the twentieth century French existentialist philosopher, recognized that in a world unmoored from absolute truth and, consequently, absolute moral standards, a person can neither claim to have greater moral insight than another nor have confidence he or she is doing the right thing. He or she must simply act.

Sartre believed a person cannot look to a pre-established belief system to decide if a certain act is morally right or wrong. In *Existentialism and Humanism*, he wrote:

The existentialist is strongly opposed to a certain type of secular moralism which seeks to suppress God at the least possible expense...In other words...nothing will be changed if God does not exist; we shall rediscover the same norms of honesty, progress and humanity, and we shall have disposed of God as an out-of-date hypothesis which will die away quietly of itself. The existentialist, on the contrary, finds it extremely embarrassing that God does not exist, for there disappears with Him all possibility of finding values in an intelligible heaven. There can no longer be any good à priori, since there is no infinite and perfect consciousness to think it. It is nowhere written that "the good" exists, that one must be honest or must not lie, since we are now upon the plane where there are only men. Dostoievsky once wrote: If God did not exist, everything would be permitted"; and that, for existentialism, is the starting point. Everything is indeed permitted if God does not exist. [2]

So, as Sartre observed, in a world without absolute truth it is impossible to condemn actions as immoral or wrong. Why? Because if there are no absolute truths, we cannot condemn another's actions as morally bad simply because we think he or she is bad.

Sartre pointed out that we cannot get rid of absolute truth and expect moral standards to survive. Without the foundation of absolute truth, we lose the ability to make ethical judgments.

If Wittgenstein is correct, we do not have intuitive or *a priori* knowledge of right and wrong because our moral ideas are taught to us by the particular society we happened to be raised in. It follows that a person raised in a society different from ours could have moral ideas radically different from our own.

Consequently, his or her actions would not be bad simply because he or she violates the moral dictates of our society. So long as he or she is following the moral stipulations of his or her society, his or her actions cannot be considered to be morally bad.

To use an example that is probably too simplistic, let us take the example of stealing cookies from the cookie jar. In our society, children are taught it is bad to take cookies from the cookie jar without permission. That is to say, we teach children the lesson that stealing is bad.

Now, imagine a person raised in a different society, who has been taught it is good to steal from the cookie jar and get away with it—this alternative society believes this teaches children to be resourceful. If the child from the alternative society steals a cookie from the cookie jar, we cannot condemn his or her actions as bad. If we do, we are merely saying we do not like the moral rules the alternative society has adopted—that our ethical rules are superior.

Children stealing cookies may seem innocent enough, but the consequences of the denial of absolute truth and the acceptance of moral relativism are more sinister. If we draw out the logical consequences of moral relativism, those who accept this theory cannot, with intellectual clarity and honesty, condemn the actions of those they believe to be wrong.

If we examine history, even of a relatively recent vintage, the disturbing nature of moral relativism becomes apparent. Hitler's attempt to systematically exterminate the Jewish people, and the institutional racism of the Southern United States during the Jim Crow era, cannot be judged as morally wrong by the moral relativist. These actions may brutally offend our sense of right and wrong, but the moral relativist cannot apply his or her values to others.

If there is no absolute right or wrong, good or bad, these heinous acts (I can state this because I do believe in absolute moral values) can only be judged within the ethical framework the particular actor has been trained into or adopted. So, if there is no absolute truth, we must judge Hitler within his moral framework. To say this is distasteful is the understatement of the century.

KILLING FREEDOM

Further, if we accept the position that truth is relative and contingent on society, we must, thereby, accept some of the most cherished ideals of post-modern liberal society originated through a series of historical accidents. So, if the results of the American Civil War or World War II had been different, certain of our values may have been obliterated.

But, don't we deeply believe that even if Hitler had triumphed and completed the mass murder of European Jews, or if the Confederacy was victorious, genocide and slavery would still be morally wrong? This is because the values we hold dear can be suppressed by oppressive regimes, but they cannot be eliminated.

But, if the contingent view of truth outlined in the previous chapter is correct, it would be possible to control free thought by controlling language. Further, if you control what people think about and you can control everyone's thoughts, you can destroy concepts like freedom and equality.

The theory behind this can be broken down in the following manner. First, ideas are dependent upon language because a person cannot hold an idea if there is no language to describe that idea. Second, language is dependent on and controlled by society. So, if one controls society, one controls language and controls ideas. If this is true, concepts like justice and freedom could be eliminated from language or remolded in ways utterly incomprehensible and disgusting to many of us.

In a world where thought is dependent on language, one cannot dream of freeing oneself or society from the shackles of the oppressor, if the oppressor has eliminated the concept of freedom. George Orwell helped us imagine such a living nightmare.

In his novel, *1984*, Orwell described a totalitarian society formed after a devastating global conflict. The world had been divided into three totalitarian states: Oceania, Eastasia, and Eurasia. The main protagonist, Winston Smith, lives in Oceania, which consists of North and South America, Australia, the British Isles, and South Africa.

The inhabitants of Oceania are divided into three groups. The *Inner Party*, the smallest group, controls Oceania. Below the *Inner Party* are members of the *Outer Party* of which Winston Smith is a member. The largest group, the *Proles*, is at the bottom of the heap.

The *Inner Party* seeks to control language and so mold society by managing the concepts of reality held by ordinary people. They have developed a language called *Newspeak* and are constantly working to improve *Newspeak* by shrinking it. Words such as liberty or freedom are either not contained in *Newspeak* or their meanings have been utterly changed.[3]

Members of the *Inner* and *Outer Parties* are indoctrinated into *Ingsoc* (an abbreviation of English Socialism), the official ideology of Oceania. The Ministry of Truth disseminates propaganda, the Ministry of Love captures and tortures anyone who exhibits unorthodox behavior, the Ministry of Peace conducts war with Oceania's enemies, and the Ministry of Plenty ensures goods are strictly rationed. In the world of *1984*, many concepts familiar to us have been turned on their heads (e.g., "war is peace").[4]

If truth is not absolute, but contingent upon societal indoctrination, then society can destroy concepts like freedom and justice just as these concepts were destroyed in Orwell's *1984*. If society teaches a language where these concepts have been eliminated or twisted beyond recognition, new members of such a society will grow up without such concepts.

If there is no word for freedom, can anyone know what freedom is? One may object that surely a more successful insurgent than Winston Smith will emerge to speak truth to power, to claim that every man is free, and so change society.

But, one lesson can be taken from *1984*. If truth is contingent upon language, a totalitarian society that successfully manipulates and molds language to its purposes could perpetuate itself forever.

Richard Rorty, one of the foremost American philosophers of recent years, acknowledged this fact. Rorty adhered to Wittgenstein's contention that thought is contingent on language and society. In his book *Contingency, Irony, and Solidarity*, Rorty articulated what the contingency of thought meant for liberal society and values. He believed that if our ideas were based on community indoctrination, the moral values of post-modern civilization were arrived at by historical accident.

In Rorty's opinion, post-modern society values freedom of conscience and abhors torture, simply because things happened to work out that way. He contended there is nothing inherent in human nature that compels the existence of such values or guarantees their endurance.

He wrote:

> ...*I do not think there are any plain moral facts out there in the world, nor any truths independent of language, nor any neutral ground on*

which to stand and argue that either torture or kindness are prefer-
able to each other.[5]

Rorty believed that if our beliefs are contingent upon language, it is possible other societies arise where acts we believe to be morally repugnant may be morally acceptable. In *Contingency, Irony, and Solidarity*, he pointed out that we could just as easily live in the world of *1984* as in the world of the Universal Declaration of Human Rights.

He wrote:

> *He [George Orwell] convinced us that there was a perfectly good*
> *chance that the same developments which had made human equality*
> *technically possible might make endless slavery possible. He did so by*
> *convincing us that nothing in the nature of truth, or man, or history*
> *was going to block that scenario, any more than it was going to under-*
> *write the scenario which liberals had been using between the wars. He*
> *convinced us that the intellectual and poetic gifts which had made*
> *Greek philosophy, modern science and Romantic poetry possible might*
> *someday find employment in the Ministry of Truth.*[6]

Rorty maintained that O'Brien, a senior member of the *Inner Party* who tortures Winston in *1984*, could not be condemned as evil because in the world envisioned by Orwell in *1984*, psychological torture was the only activity in which gifted intellectuals (who if things had worked out differently might have been liberal arts college professors) could find intellectual satisfaction. In a world where the *Inner Party*—by means of its grip on language and society—has destroyed any aspirations to human freedom (even in thought) the idea of a liberal intellectual is not just impossible—it is incomprehensible.

How could O'Brien work to further liberty and justice as we conceive of them if these concepts no longer existed? It would make as much sense for him to try to study the existence of unicorns.

If Wittgenstein and Rorty are correct, we live in a world where a warped society can change moral values as it sees fit through systematic control of language. More disturbing is the fact that we cannot condemn such a warped society as that of Oceania in 1984 as wrong or evil.

In fact, if we were to be socialized into such a society, we would (by necessity) do things that we, from our current vantage point, would consider morally repugnant. We would not be choosing to commit bad actions, but our socialization would not present us with any choice.

Furthermore, it is also possible that values we consider as sacred in post-modern liberal society might cease to exist. If we deny the existence of absolute truth and embrace a relative theory of truth, we must be prepared to accept the demise of some of the most cherished ideals of post-modern civilization.

The next chapter argues we are not prepared to accept that the denial of the existence of absolute truth entails the possible future destruction of the human spirit.

Where I Agree With Wittgenstein

Ludwig Wittgenstein was undoubtedly one of the greatest, if not *the* greatest philosopher of the twentieth century. So far I have attempted to convince you that his theory that truth is contingent upon social indoctrination is mistaken. However, that is not to say that there are not parts of his thinking that I agree with. And, it would be foolish to dismiss the output of such a brilliant mind in its entirety.

Wittgenstein argued it was nonsensical to contend language be entirely subjective and internal. In *Philosophical Investigations*, he contended that if everyone had their own individual language and, therefore, their own concepts and ideas, this would not be a language at all.[7] No one could communicate if we all had different words for the same thing. In other words, for a language to be a language at least two people must share it. Language and our concepts are shared—they are public and objective, not private and subjective.

Wittgenstein's private language argument was designed to counter the problem of the existence of other minds. A traditional problem in philosophy, related to whether one can prove the existence of the external physical world, is whether we can prove the existence of minds other than our own.

As explained in Chapter 2, this was a particular problem for the Empiricists. Wittgenstein and others, such as Martin Heidegger, rejected these skeptical problems as non-problems that arose from a mistaken philosophical outlook. Instead of focusing on how concepts or ideas occur in our own minds, Wittgenstein contended we needed to engage these ideas at the level we encounter them in our everyday reality. There is no need to look for something behind the everyday.

If truth is absolute, truth must be public and capable of being shared by more than one person. Otherwise, absolute truth cannot be universal. Wittgenstein was correct in recognizing that to escape the skeptical problems that had entangled philosophy, we must have public and not private concepts of truth.

He placed the origin of these public concepts in community indoctrination. However, as I have repeatedly stated, a theory of truth based on social indoctrination raises more questions than answers. Hence, the realization truth must be public and not private was a major step forward.

CHAPTER FOUR

CAN WE BELIEVE IN UNIVERSAL HUMAN RIGHTS & MORAL RELATIVISM SIMULTANEOUSLY?

Whereas recognition of the inherent dignity and of the equal and inalienable rights of all members of the human family is the foundation of freedom, justice and peace in the world..."

—PREAMBLE TO THE UNIVERSAL DECLARATION OF HUMAN RIGHTS[1]

While the twentieth century witnessed a growing acceptance of relative truth and moral relativism, it also saw a consensus emerge from the horrors of that bloody century that certain rights are universal and absolute. This chapter examines a contradiction at the heart of post-modern civilization: how do human rights theory and law work in a world without absolute truth?

As World War II waned and the Allied powers drove farther into German-controlled territory, the full extent of the genocidal crimes of Hitler's Germany became apparent. Hitler's attempt to exterminate the Jewish people as if they were animals to be slaughtered shocked the world. The massive mobilization and organization of a modern state and its citizens to obliterate those who were different was horrifying. There was a sense that the actions of Hitler's Germany were a stain on the conscience of humanity that could not be left unpunished.

The United States, the United Kingdom, France and the Soviet Union established the Nuremberg Tribunal to try high-ranking Nazis for war crimes and crimes against humanity. The individuals tried at Nuremberg committed their crimes under the cover of, and with the blessing of, the German government—they *were* the German government.

For the first time in history, individuals were tried for crimes against humanity.[2] The high-ranking Nazi Party members before the court at Nuremberg were not being tried by their own state, Germany, but by the world community.

A state like Nazi Germany could not be trusted to try its own members for actions the government authorized and facilitated. Therefore, other states stepped in to ensure individual human rights were vindicated by punishing those who violated these rights. This was a new idea. Previously, it was thought that individuals could only be tried and punished by the states to which they were subject. However, after the end of World War II, it was believed some crimes were so heinous they could not go unpunished if a particular state was unwilling to bring its own citizens to justice for such crimes. This was the genesis of the idea that, because human rights are universal, any judicial system (even one located in a state far from where the crimes were committed) can try individuals for human rights violations. This developed into the concept of universal jurisdiction.[3]

The defendants at Nuremberg argued that international law could only punish states and not individuals, but the Nuremberg Court rejected this defense.[4] The Nuremberg Court held that individuals could be punished for crimes against humanity under international law. This was the beginning of human rights law as we think of it in the twenty-first century.

After Nuremberg, the development of human rights law and institutions to enforce these rights continued to gather speed. The twentieth century saw tribunals established to try war crimes committed in the former Yugoslavia and Rwanda.[5] On July 17, 1998, 120 nations voted to adopt the Rome Statute, leading to the establishment of the International Criminal Court to try individuals for genocide, war crimes, and crimes against humanity.[6]

Parallel to the development of international judicial bodies to punish human rights violations was the move to clearly embody human rights norms in written texts. On December 10, 1948, the General Assembly of the United Nations adopted and proclaimed the Universal Declaration of Human Rights.

The Universal Declaration of Human Rights states every person has the "right to life, liberty and security of person," freedom from slavery, freedom from "torture" or "cruel, inhuman or degrading treatment or punishment," among other rights.[7] The assumption underlying the Universal Declaration of Human Rights is that certain rights are common to all mankind and should not be abridged.

The Universal Declaration of Human Rights did not, however, arise fully-formed out of a vacuum. It echoed previous landmark texts that had arisen out of tumultuous events such as Jefferson's Declaration of Independence and the Declaration of the Rights of Man of the French Revolution. The Universal Declaration of Human Rights was proclaimed to a world severely scarred by global conflict and the horrors of genocide during World War II. It was also a world that had witnessed the Nuremberg trials.

Ask anyone why every person should have the right to life, liberty, and security of person, or why slavery is wrong. The answer one would most likely receive from a great number of people is that the rights enumerated in the Universal Declaration of Human Rights are universal and absolute. How do we know this? Is this intuitive or a priori knowledge we somehow possess? It is difficult to conceive of another adequate response to this question.

If the assumption that certain human rights are universal is incorrect, the Universal Declaration of Human Rights is meaningless. If truth is contingent upon societal indoctrination as contended by Wittgenstein and Rorty, the assumption underlying the Universal Declaration of Human Rights is incorrect.

If there are no absolute truths, there can be no universal human rights. If there are no absolute truths and our concepts of justice, freedom, and peace are contingent upon our cultural and historical position, the assumption everyone shares the same ideas about freedom, justice, and peace cannot be justified.

As we saw in the previous chapter, if truth is contingent upon the society in which we live, we must accept that the values of post-modern liberal civilization are essentially an historical accident. There is nothing intuitive or universally or absolutely true about freedom from torture or freedom from slavery; our society just happens to have come up with these values over time.

Even more alarming—if we accept the contingent theory of truth—a society could be created in which concepts like freedom could be destroyed or twisted beyond recognition. In Orwell's *1984*, freedom is synonymous with slavery[8] because the *Inner Party* has manipulated language and society to make it so. Therefore, if truth and moral values are relative, one cannot claim that certain human rights are universally applicable to all cultures and all people.

Nazi Germany developed a fascist ideology justifying the denial of fundamental human rights to certain ethnic groups. In Hitler's Germany, Auschwitz was acceptable and morally justifiable. The Nuremberg defendants had been indoctrinated, and had indoctrinated others, into the twisted ideology of National Socialism.

Like the world Orwell created in *1984*, Germany (between 1933 and 1945) was a society in which moral concepts had been twisted and manipulated. If the defendants at Nuremberg had argued they should not be convicted for crimes against humanity because the victorious Allied powers were imposing moral values on them that as Nazi Party members they did not share, we would have been incredulous and outraged.

However, if there are no absolute truths, they could have plausibly argued there was no such thing as a crime against humanity. In that case, what was a crime in the United States or the United Kingdom would be a moral judgment specific to *that* society, not necessarily a crime in Nazi Germany. In effect, labeling an act as a crime against humanity would merely be the victor imposing the relative truths and values of its society on the vanquished.

To claim universal human rights exist is to claim that certain actions are wrong in all societies at all times. No society can claim these universal rights do not apply to it or its citizens. Neither can a society destroy these rights. It is to claim that fundamental human rights exist apart from society—they just are.

No matter how a society like Nazi Germany attempts to indoctrinate its citizens, no one has the right to torture or enslave another human being. Therefore, a universal system of human rights depends on the existence of absolute truth if it is to make any intellectual sense. So, if absolute truth is jettisoned, modern human rights law must also be abandoned.

Perhaps it can be argued that everyone shares the same concepts of freedom, justice, and peace because the entire human race has been culturally indoctrinated into these concepts. This would mean human rights are not absolute and universal and only appear to be because all communities teach their members to accept these concepts.

But, the community-based theory of the origin of ideas expounded by Wittgenstein, Rorty, and others is still fatal to a universal declaration of human rights. If it is possible for a human society to emerge with no concept of freedom, justice, or peace—or with an idea of these concepts so different from our current understanding so as to be unrecognizable——the universal application of these concepts cannot be maintained.

Why? Because, if that were the case, it would only be by chance that we treat fundamental human rights as universal, and a community that did not happen to share our penchant for respecting these rights could not be condemned as wrong or immoral. Moreover, the existence of societies such as Nazi Germany gives the lie to the fact that everyone shares the same moral concepts through cultural indoctrination.

SPEAKING TRUTH TO POWER

In the world of *1984*, human rights, such as freedom of thought and expression, had been eradicated. Winston Smith's struggle to rebel against the post-totalitarian society of Oceania ultimately failed. Winston could not maintain his belief that the world would be better off without *Big Brother*. In the face of torture, he became convinced the only truth was what the *Inner Party* wanted him to believe.

If truth is contingent and reality can be manipulated as it was in *1984*, we have to accept the concept of human rights could be destroyed by a totalitarian society that controlled language. On the other hand, if there are universal *a priori* human rights, no society could ever truly eliminate the existence of these rights. Individuals would always just know torturing or enslaving human beings was wrong.

In the twentieth century, a number of totalitarian societies emerged that fiercely regulated the freedom of their citizens. However, dissidents arose and refused to accept that human rights did not apply to them. From the October Revolution in 1917 until the collapse of the Soviet Union in the late 1980s and early 1990s, the Communist Party sought to impose its ideology on all inhabitants of the Soviet Union to the extent of crushing even potential threats to its dominance. The legitimacy and effectiveness of Communist Party rule was to be beyond question. Those who dared question, and many more for no better reason than it suited the authorities, were executed or exiled to brutal labor camps in Siberia. There was sometimes a show of judicial proceeding to justify punishment; although, more often than not, offenders were arrested, tortured into a confession of their alleged crimes, and punished.

Whole ethnic groups were collectively punished. The Communist Party controlled by fear; no one could be sure they were safe from arrest. Even former senior Communist Party members were not immune from such summary justice. Freedom of movement and association were controlled and curtailed by the Communist Party.

Failure to denounce others for the myriad acts or omissions considered crimes against the motherland was a crime punishable by exile to Siberia. It is well known that Orwell was targeting the totalitarian regime of the Soviet Union for criticism in *1984*.

In spite of the purges, summary executions, and exiles to Siberia, the Communist Party did not successfully strangle all dissent. Even time in the labor camps of Siberia did not silence its critics.

Alexander Solzhenitsyn spent many years in the Soviet gulags. As a writer, he described the evil underbelly of the Soviet system, both in fictional and factual works, in order to expose it to the world outside of the Soviet Union. In particular, his book, *The Gulag Archipelago*, detailed the history and workings of the labor camps the Soviet security system used against its citizens.[9] He chronicled the personal and epic nature of the attempt by the authorities to maintain ideological and physical control over the inhabitants of the geographically sprawling Soviet Union.

Solzhenitsyn succeeded in reality where Winston Smith failed in the fictional *1984*. He never erred in his contention that he was on the side of right. He was the archetypical intellectual "speaking truth to power." He had only his intellect, his writing, and the conviction that the truth must be told to challenge the crushing might of the Soviet Empire and its labyrinth of secret police and prisons – but he succeeded.

His words had, and still have, power. His writing contributed to the further decline of any legitimacy the Soviet Union may have clung to in the eyes of sympathizers in the world not stifled by the Iron Curtain.

We like to think individuals like Solzhenitsyn, Reverend Martin Luther King, Jr. or Mahatma Gandhi will always rise up in repressive societies to remind people of their inherent rights to freedom and dignity. Whistleblowers who expose the misdeeds of giant corporations or government bureaucracies are lauded in our society, and often become the heroes of popular movies.[10]

But, if one accepts the contingent theory of truth, one would have to further accept that a society like the one Orwell described in *1984* could exist, and that if such a society successfully manipulated language and technology, its existence would be permanent. No dissident could rise up and speak truth to power and cry out for freedom. Freedom as we know it would not be a concept that could be conceived in such a society. No Solzhenitsyn or Reverend Martin Luther King, Jr. would arise to speak out against oppression and "speak truth to power."

In *1984*, Winston Smith wanted to destroy the system constraining his movements both physically and mentally. He was isolated, and before he met his lover Julia, he was not sure if anyone shared his antipathy towards the *Inner Party*.

Winston's struggle was more difficult than merely locating potential fellow insurgents to aid in the overthrow of the regime. Due to the monopoly on every means of disseminating information and the constant alteration of the past to comply with the *Inner Party*'s needs, he had difficulty imagining a world without *Big Brother*.

Indoctrination told him the world had been a terrible place, run by evil capitalists, that was rescued by *Ingsoc*, or English Socialism. The official *Inner Party* line was that citizens of Oceania had a better quality of life with more to eat and more comfort after the revolution. Winston doubted this, and knew that many of the economic and agricultural statistics generated by the *Inner Party* to evidence how well things are going were pure fiction. In fact, Winston's job often entailed the creation of such fanciful statistics.

Winston was a child at the time of the revolution, so he tried to draw on childhood memories of his mother and younger sister to convince himself that life before *Ingsoc* was better than the world in which he found himself. He also tried to consult elderly *Proles* who had not been subject to the same intensive indoctrination as party members.

However, Winston could not fully convince himself life would be better without *Big Brother* and the *Inner Party*. He could not use his mind as a repository of fact to store evidence that he could present to indict the regime in the courtroom of his mind. His vague memories of his childhood and family did not carry the day for him—he needed tangible proof his beliefs were not mistaken.

The memories of the elderly *Proles* were of no help either. They could not provide Winston with meaningful details of the past, either because of propaganda or senility. It was only as he briefly held in his hands documentary evidence of the duplicity of the *Inner Party* that he really allowed himself to dare to doubt the regime.

In the course of his duties in the Ministry of Information, he came across a newspaper extract and picture showing three former prominent leaders of the *Inner Party* who had been denounced as traitors for collaborating with Oceania's enemies. The newspaper clipping was significant because it showed these alleged traitors in New York at an *Inner Party* function on the same date they were supposedly conspiring with the enemy.

It exposed the falsity of *Inner Party* propaganda. After reading this clipping, he immediately destroyed it, afraid *Big Brother* would punish him. At times when he wanted to reinforce his opposition to the status quo, he recalled this brief handling of tangible indictment of the system.

His opposition was further reinforced when O'Brien—a member of the *Inner Party* posing as a dissident to trap Winston—gave Winston a copy of a text supposedly written by an arch-dissident. This particular volume was instead written by O'Brien and other members of the *Inner Party* to lay another level of disinformation.

Winston needed written proof to validate his opposition to the *Inner Party*. In the fictional world of *1984*, thought was dependent upon language. Therefore, Winston could not maintain independent thoughts at variance with the constant barrage of *Inner Party* propaganda. Any vestige of independent thought Winston possessed was destroyed after he was tortured in the Ministry of Love. He was permanently broken.

He had not momentarily given in so the torture would stop—a weakness he would later regret or rationalize. He surrendered. He would no longer fight to establish sovereignty over his mind; he had accepted that truth was whatever *Big Brother* said it was, no matter how inconsistent.

Contrast this with the real-life example of Alexander Solzhenitsyn who lived in the Soviet Union under a regime constantly seeking to mold reality using propaganda. Information was strictly controlled, and anyone who may potentially threaten the status quo was exiled or killed.

Solzhenitsyn was exiled to the gulags, but never lost his conviction that the actions of Communist Party leadership were wrong. That it was wrong to arbitrarily deprive citizens of liberty without meaningful and impartial judicial proceedings. That it was wrong to torture prisoners into sham confessions and accuse the blameless of criminal wrongdoings for trying to exercise intellectual freedom. That it was morally wrong to execute citizens solely because it was expedient for those in power to do so. Again, Solzhenitsyn succeeded in real life where the fictional Winston failed.

However, if truth is dependent upon cultural indoctrination, and culture is strictly controlled, the advent of dissenters such as Solzhenitsyn would be impossible. There is no doubt the Soviet Union went quite far along the road of establishing cultural dominance over its citizens, but while dissidents could be silenced or forced to confess, their internal opposition to the regime could not be eliminated.

We would think it ridiculous to accept the impossibility of dissident voices rising up to criticize repressive regimes. Isn't it natural for voices to challenge morally corrupt regimes from within? However, if truth is relative, a repressive society like that portrayed in 1984 could come about in which dissent would be not just impossible, but utterly inconceivable.

If, after reading this chapter you scream, "No, I believe in the sacredness of equality and liberty, and the existence of universal human rights!" you cannot logically hold a contingent theory of truth and moral relativism. To do so would be contradictory.

One who believes in universal human rights and the contingency of truth is merely imposing his or her subjective views about human rights on other people. How can we claim certain human rights such as freedom from slavery are universal if we do not believe in universal truths?

Further, if we accept that truth is contingent upon societal indoctrination, we must logically accept that concepts like freedom and equality could disappear or be changed into something quite different. We must accept that the tradition of speaking truth to power is also contingent upon social indoctrination and so is not guaranteed to persist.

Therefore, the only consistent position an advocate for human rights can take is to affirm the existence of absolute moral truth and, consequently, absolute truth. Otherwise, one cannot condemn even the most heinous of crimes against humanity with intellectual honesty and consistency.

If we accept the existence of absolute universal truth, we have to examine how we came to know these absolute truths. This brings us back to Plato and his theory of the Forms. If we wish to vehemently defend the existence of universal human rights, do we return to positing a reality outside of our everyday world where these universal truths exist?

Philosophers have struggled to free themselves from metaphysical speculation about the origin of absolute truth. Perhaps the reason a satisfactory answer cannot be found to explain our moral ideas evidences the fact that the escape from metaphysics is itself the problem.

CHAPTER FIVE

THE CONTINGENCY CONTRADICTION

"A house divided against itself cannot stand."

—ABRAHAM LINCOLN[1]

In previous chapters, I explained that the acceptance of relative truth entails many unpleasant consequences. We lose the ability to morally question the actions of others. Additionally, because the existence of universal human rights is inconsistent with a relative theory of truth, modern human rights law cannot be enforced with intellectual consistency.

Further, we must logically accept that if some of our most cherished concepts such as freedom are contingent, there is no guarantee these concepts will always exist. Having said this, there is, perhaps, a more serious objection to the theory that truth is contingent or relative. This theory contradicts itself and, if examined closely, actually argues for the existence of absolute truth.

If truth is relative and there are no absolute truths, how do we know the statement *all truth is relative* is true? This statement claims to be true in all circumstances—no matter what, truth is relative. In other words, this statement claims that ultimate reality consists of relative truths. So, the statement *all truth is relative* is claiming to be absolutely true.

However, if all truth is relative, the statement *all truth is relative* cannot be true in all circumstances. This is a contradiction at the heart of the theory that truth is relative because in order for this theory to be true, one must assume the existence of at least one absolute truth—that all truth is relative. If we make this assumption, then we cannot claim absolute truth does not exist.

If all truth is contingent upon social indoctrination, the theory advanced by thinkers like Wittgenstein and Rorty that truth is contingent is simply another contingent truth that just happens to be true as a result of the social and historical antecedents of post-modern society. So, it seems that those philosophers who sought to solve the problems of philosophy by abandoning absolute truth have not been entirely successful in escaping its clutches.

Therefore, to even believe that truth is contingent upon social indoctrination, one must assume the existence of absolute truth. If there is no absolute truth, the statement *all truth is contingent* is only true if social indoctrination has led us to believe it to be true. So, it may be true for one group of people and false for another group. As I have argued, this renders it essentially useless as a theory that can be applied to all humankind.

The fact that one must assume the existence of absolute truth, even to deny it exists, shows how difficult it is to say anything without assuming the existence of absolute truth. Is it possible to ever say anything meaningful if absolute truth does not exist?

Many of our beliefs depend on the existence of absolute truth. Without absolute truth, nothing we say or think can have universal application, which makes theorizing difficult, if not impossible. If any theory is only relatively true, then it can be rejected because it is true or false depending upon one's social indoctrination.

What then can be said or thought if all truth is relative? The scientist often occupies in post-modern society the role that has more traditionally been played by the priest.[2] We look to science and scientists to provide us with truth about our world and ourselves. If science, through empirical research, discovers something about the world around us, doesn't this discovery provide us with absolute truth about the universe?

We do not argue that a discovery about the nature of gravity which has been empirically proven is not absolutely true. Science presumes there are right and wrong answers concerning the ultimate nature of reality out there to be found. We would not respect the results of scientific research if it came up with answers only relatively true in certain circumstances.

If all truth is relative, then every theory—be it physics, economics, or sociology—would be true and false at the same time because the truth of a theory would depend upon whether we, through cultural indoctrination, accepted it as true or false. We could never make any statement that has universal application.

In fact, science would lose its usefulness if it did not provide answers that are absolutely true. The appeal of science is that it provides answers we can trust because they have been empirically tested.

Therefore, if all truth is relative, we can never say anything about anything. But, this is not how we conduct ourselves. In many fields of human endeavor, we constantly try to break new ground by making discoveries that reveal something new about reality.

The truths of science, be it *hard* sciences (e.g., physics or biology) or *soft* sciences (e.g., economics or sociology), are accepted as true in an absolute sense, not in a relative sense. That is not to say that every scientific theory is absolutely true, because scientific discovery is a gradual process; we may not arrive at the correct answer right away in all cases. But, instead to state that the theories and explanations of science strive to be true in an absolute sense that provides insight about the ultimate nature of reality. Indeed, history provides many examples of scientific theories once thought to be unassailably true that have been superseded by later discoveries. Why do we accept the relativity of truth when it comes to moral questions, but not in other fields of human discovery such as science?

Moreover, moral truths are arguably more fundamental and important than scientific questions. As science increasingly provides us with knowledge of our physical world, and we harness this knowledge in technological innovations, moral questions arise. Technology provides the ability to do X, but is it good to do X?

Scientific discovery can teach us to split the atom, but it cannot tell us what applications of this technology are morally permissible. Scientists can clone animals and possibly humans, but it doesn't mean that they should.

Even if we imagine a future in which science has reached the mythical end of inquiry, will moral questions and issues have disappeared? In an important sense, scientific truths are subservient to moral truth.

Until we arrive at some conclusions concerning the exercise of the scientific discoveries, the application of these discoveries will be delayed. So, if we will not permit scientists to content themselves with the pursuit of relative truth, it makes little sense to prohibit the moral philosopher from seeking absolute answers to questions essential not only to everyday life but to the scientific project itself.

If all other truths about human existence are absolute, should we maintain that moral truths are special or less privileged? Does it make sense for certain aspects of our reality to be absolutely true and others merely relatively true?

A contingent or relative theory of truth applied to science renders science useless, and, as argued in earlier chapters, a relative theory of truth applied to moral questions renders the universal application of moral standards (like the Universal Declaration of Human Rights) useless. Hence, a relative theory of truth should be abandoned as unworkable.

In light of the fact that we treat scientific truths that have a claim to empirical verification as attempts to arrive at absolute truth, this book is essentially limited to a defense of absolute moral truth. Absolute truth is accepted except when it comes to moral questions. But, these are some of the most important questions of all.

Why do we accept that science can provide us with absolute truth but deny the existence of absolute truth on moral questions? Even scientific theories which may not have been empirically tested are held to be true and to, in some way, further our knowledge of reality.

Is it because we are comfortable with answers that can be explained by factual observances and do not have to engage in metaphysics—because it is embarrassing for the educated twenty-first century citizen of the post-modern world to engage in metaphysical speculation? Why do we reject metaphysics out of hand? I believe there is an entrenched reluctance to accept the validity of metaphysical speculation because of where it might lead—to the acceptance of something like Plato's Forms or a supreme omnipresent being as the source of absolute moral truth.

In our haste to abandon *superstitions*, such as God, that may arise from metaphysical speculation into the origin of absolute moral truths, we are perhaps ignoring the fact that it may make more sense to accept the existence of absolute moral truth than to reject it. Moral questions are arguably the most important issues faced by humankind, but by accepting a contingent theory of moral truth, we are prohibiting useful answers to moral questions.

If reason directs one to accept the existence of absolute truth, one should follow its lead. Additionally, if absolute truth exists, it must have a source, and we should attempt to discover the source as this will shed more light on the nature of absolute truth itself.

CHAPTER SIX

RE-IMAGINING REALITY

"If God did not exist, it would be necessary to invent Him."

—VOLTAIRE[1]

I f you have come this far with me and have concluded you cannot accept that all of our moral concepts are contingent upon cultural and community indoctrination, the next logical step is to agree that there must be a source of absolute truth. The traditional answer arrived at has been God.

But if you are not willing to accept the existence of an absolute God as the source of absolute truth and, therefore, of absolute moral standards, another source for these absolute truths must be found. The divine option is still open, but many learned members of post-modern civilization are embarrassed to turn to the *policeman in the sky.*

As I argued in Chapter 5, when we dig down, no one truly maintains there are no absolute truths; rather, many in our post-modern world contend there are no absolute truths concerning moral or ethical questions. Many people are happy with absolute truths of the scientist, but not those of the moral philosopher. But, as argued in previous chapters, more often than not, we act like there are also absolute moral truths.

Empiricist philosophers and twentieth century philosophers of language like Wittgenstein and Rorty can be said to share a common motivation—the rejection of metaphysics. Pure speculation about a world, above or beyond the everyday world in which we strive, was abandoned as primitive superstition.

Traditionally, individuals engaged in philosophical activity could attempt to discover the nature of the Form of *Good* or *Beauty*, which existed somewhere beyond everyday experience. But no objective proof could be offered for the existence of Plato's Forms. Consequently, such metaphysical speculation became increasingly embarrassing as more and more answers concerning the world around us were provided by science.

The Empiricists, as we have previously seen, looked to sensory perception to provide objective facts about ultimate reality. Unfortunately, Empiricism led to serious skeptical problems such as the inability to prove the existence of the external world or other minds. Twentieth century philosophers such as Wittgenstein took another approach. They completely abandoned any attempt to discover grand philosophical systems to explain all. Instead, they contended that if enough people held something to be true, it was true. As this book has set out in previous chapters, this view is self-contradictory and prevents us from ever morally disapproving of the actions of others—no matter how heinous.

The starting position of Wittgenstein's later philosophy was that absolute moral truths that could only be accessed by metaphysical speculation could not exist. This position was adopted, not because the existence of absolute moral truths had been disproved (such truths are not amenable to being proved or disproved), but as a form of superstitious nonsense. But, was the only tenable theory that explained the nature of our moral ideas abandoned because of a prejudice against metaphysics?

We examined the theory that moral truths are relative or contingent upon society and found this theory wanting in several respects. If truth is contingent, actions cannot be condemned in moral terms, and cherished ideas such as freedom and equality are dependent for their continued existence on society.

We have also seen how this theory contradicts itself, as the statement *all truth is contingent on society* makes a claim to be absolutely true. In addition, we noted that we do not permit the outputs of science to be relatively true. Moreover, by accepting the existence of universal human rights and adopting international legal documents to articulate and enforce them, we demonstrate, in practical terms, that much of what we believe to be modern liberal democracy is built upon an assumption of the existence of objective absolute moral truths.

So, it seems Rorty and Wittgenstein (at least in his later philosophy) failed to formulate a satisfactory explanation of the origin of moral ideas. If there is no better alternative to the existence of absolute moral truths, should we accept the existence of absolute moral truths and abandon prejudices that blindly reject the existence of absolute moral truth as a first principle?

We trust the answers provided by science, or at least the legitimacy of the scientific project, because of the objective and verifiable nature of the scientific endeavor. Science has been successful in providing answers and it is a great temptation to apply the scientific method to more fields of study for this reason. This temptation ensnared the Empiricist philosophers. However, there are places science cannot travel and questions it cannot answer.

For example, scientists cannot provide us with answers to moral questions or, at least, answers to satisfy those that cling to the universality of certain truths. Can science tell us what *good* is or whether it is ever right to torture someone?

No facts can answer these questions; a moral framework for judging these questions is required. Indeed, as I argued in Chapter 5, often the pursuit of scientific discovery and the application of these discoveries raises moral questions that need to be addressed before the scientific experiment or the harnessing of technological advances can proceed. This shows that science cannot replace moral inquiry and will always be subject to it.

Plato believed philosophers could try to discover the meanings behind our ideas (what he called the Forms), but many philosophers who followed in his wake have recognized the limits of the ability of the human mind, whether through metaphysics or science, to uncover the ultimate furniture of the universe. Some philosophers who have attempted to search for truth without resorting to metaphysics have discovered they had to scale back the ambition of their aims or abandon the big money questions altogether.

Two celebrated philosophers concluded ultimate truths about the universe were beyond human reason and investigation and, so, beyond the philosopher and the scientist. German philosopher Immanuel Kant concluded we could never reach out to grab answers to the great metaphysical questions, and Wittgenstein, in his early philosophical career, held that these questions could only be touched by engaging in some sort of mysticism.

Kant argued that it was impossible for humans to ever know ultimate reality. He believed we perceive everything in space and time because of the way the human mind is constructed. However, Kant contended that ultimate reality exists outside of space and time. Since we cannot perceive anything outside of space and time, we cannot know or discover ultimate reality of *things in themselves*, but only *things as they appear to us*.[2] So, according to Kant, neither the scientist nor the philosopher can provide us with the answer of what is ultimately out there.

Ludwig Wittgenstein, in what scholars label his early period, asserted that philosophers could untangle certain philosophical problems but could not develop elaborate theories about ultimate reality. In his first major philosophical work, *Tractatus Logico-Philosophicus* (and in fact his only philosophical work published while he was alive), he argued philosophers should stop attempting to use metaphysical ladders to discover the ultimate secrets of the universe.

In the *Tractatus*, Wittgenstein's aim was to describe the limits of what could be sensibly said using language. He asserted that language can only make logical and factual claims, and could not say anything meaningful about subjects like morality or religion. He maintained there were two types of propositions that could be meaningfully discussed. First, logical propositions, which he stated were tautologies, which means these propositions are necessarily true in and of themselves, but do not provide us with new information about the world. Second, propositions that can be empirically verified, which fall under the province of the natural sciences.

Philosophical propositions concerned with ethical truths, and truths about ultimate reality, do not fit into either of these categories. They are neither logical tautologies nor empirically verifiable propositions. Therefore, Wittgenstein asserted that moral statements could not be verified by human reason or experience. Concerning such propositions he wrote:

"…whereof one cannot speak, one must remain silent."[3]

Some of Wittgenstein's contemporaries, in particular the philosophical movement known as the *Vienna Circle*, took Wittgenstein to mean that propositions that were not logical tautologies or that could not be empirically verified were meaningless, but another reading of the Tractatus leads one to conclude that Wittgenstein held the unverifiable propositions to be more meaningful. He was merely trying to point out that propositions such as "X is good" or "Y is beautiful" could not be discovered by science or philosophy.

He held that the fact that there was a logical structure to language showed there was more to reality, but this *something more* could not be analyzed according to human logic and reasoning. Wittgenstein asserted that such propositions about the ultimate nature of reality could be, in his words, *shown* but not *said*. He wrote:

"There is indeed the inexpressible. This shows itself; it is the mystical."[4]

According to this reading, the Wittgenstein of the *Tractatus* held that there were important truths about ultimate reality which could not be captured by the language of philosophy or science. Further support for this view can be gleaned from correspondence between Wittgenstein and Ludwig von Ficker, the publisher of *Tractatus*.

Wittgenstein wrote to von Ficker that there were two parts to the *Tractatus* and he had left out the more important part.[5] In addition, in the preface to the *Tractatus*, Wittgenstein revealed he was interested in plotting the limits of language because only then could one discover what lay beyond it. He wanted to solve philosophical problems by proving that such problems arose because of the inherent limits of language. After the logical analysis of the *Tractatus* was complete, philosophical problems would be shown to be meaningless. However, Wittgenstein contended that after this analysis was complete, very little progress had been made.

Wittgenstein's early philosophical views encapsulated in the *Tractatus* make a lot of sense. Philosophical problems, such as how we know what the *good* is, cannot be logically determined in a scientific or philosophical manner. Ever since Plato's theory of the Forms was rejected by thinkers attempting to provide answers to philosophical questions solely using scientific methods, philosophy has been tied up in knots.

Empiricist philosophers tried to limit their investigations to knowledge obtained from sensory perception and ended up questioning the reality of the world around them, including the existence of other minds. The logical positivists rejected everything, except logical tautologies and empirically-verifiable statements as nonsense. Statements about morality had no meanings for them. This was surely a ridiculous position. Much of human life and behavior would be annihilated if the logical positivists were correct. Twentieth century ordinary language philosophers, led by Wittgenstein (in his later period), recognized that the solution of the logical positivists was untenable.

A satisfactory philosophical theory of truth cannot reject all statements other than logical tautologies as rubbish, because such statements are part of the essential fabric of human existence. Instead, these twentieth century philosophers asserted that truth was contingent on community indoctrination.

As we have seen, they contended that philosophical problems vanished when one realized all truth is relative and contingent upon community indoctrination. However, as we have also discovered, the contingent view of truth has inherent flaws that render it intellectually unacceptable for anyone who holds any remote hope of escaping utter despair.

If one desires to hold that there are universal norms of human behavior, such as those enumerated in the Universal Declaration of Human Rights, one cannot with a straight face adhere to a contingent theory of truth after a serious and honest examination.

So, where does this leave us? Back where we started, with Plato and his theory of the Forms? I believe so.

As an undergraduate student of philosophy, I was repeatedly cautioned against use of the verb *to believe* in my class papers. Instead of stating that I, or a particular philosopher, *believed*, I was instructed to write *held, asserted,* or *contended.* The verb *to believe* had unpleasant metaphysical and, in particular, religious associations. A philosopher did not base his or her work on belief. So it is with this cautionary advice in mind that I state I believe so, for I believe that even though it is clear to me that absolute truths exist, it is also clear these truths cannot be examined or discovered in a scientific or logical way. We must accept that these absolute truths transcend us and the particular culture in which we find ourselves.

Why are we so reluctant to accept a transcendent theory of truth if after examination it is the theory that provides the best explanation of truth? The big problem is, if we accept a transcendent theory of truth, which is the only theory that fits with an embrace of absolute ideas, we are accepting the existence of a metaphysical realm like where Plato's Forms reside—perhaps swinging open a door to the acceptance of belief in an omnipresent deity. But such metaphysical beliefs are an intellectual no-no for many thinkers. Any theory that could end up in acceptance of a metaphysical realm, or God, must be rejected as absurd.

It is contended that such beliefs amount to little more than the residue of primitive human beliefs lingering from pre-scientific times. But, we have seen that the attempt to sidestep absolute truth and, therefore, avoid a transcendent view of truth, has led to unsustainable philosophical issues.

What if it makes more logical sense to accept the existence of absolute truth and to further accept that the source of these truths is independent of ourselves and our communities? Shouldn't an unbiased person weighing these issues accept the existence of absolute truth that we can somehow access, but which is beyond the everyday?

The point of this book is to argue that an honest review of these issues inevitably ends at this position. The problem is many people are clouded by certain philosophical prejudices that prevent a straightforward and open examination of the nature of truth.

If we take as a starting point that the existence of a metaphysical realm is absurd, of course we will end up rejecting absolute truth. But, we should ensure our starting point is justified, not based on prejudice.

If we reject the existence of the metaphysical or the transcendent as the starting point of inquiry, of course we will reject transcendent absolute values. But to begin from such a position is not to step onto the path of honest and open discovery. I would argue the reason that philosophy has ended up in such a muddle is precisely because of the rejection of the transcendent as a source of ideas or truth.

The Empiricists wanted to put knowledge on the sounder footing of sensory perception—something concrete and tangible; the logical positivists, on empirically verifiable propositions and logical tautologies, which, by their very nature, must be true. Finally, the ordinary language philosophers of the twentieth century attempted to base truth on culture. All of these philosophical movements had the rejection of the transcendent as a common factor. However, another common feature that all of them share is that none of them adequately account for human morality or what I call the human rights urge.

Only an absolute theory of truth can explain the acceptance of a universal legal human rights system birthed from the revulsion of the brutal inhumanity of the death camps of the Second World War II. As we have seen, the existence of absolute values must exist outside of us and society because otherwise these values could not be universal.

So, we are presented with a stark choice. Either reject the transcendent, and with it any possibility of ever condemning the actions of others on moral grounds, or embrace the norms of international human rights laws and the absolute truths that must underlay these norms, and thereby, embrace the possibility that the source of absolute truth is transcendent. Any other choice is intellectually confused and—after a serious review of the issues—intellectually dishonest.

If science cannot provide us with answers to questions about absolute moral truths, we must look elsewhere—to the transcendent. If you reject this move as an unscientific "leap of faith" you must recognize that by accepting the Universal Declaration of Human Rights you have already made this move.

Those who believe in the divine as the source of absolute truth are often derided as primitive, irrational, and superstitious. On the other hand, no one has arrived at a theory that explains absolute truth adequately without recourse to the supernatural. So perhaps, belief in God is primary and not primitive.

Of course it can be argued that eventually science will discover all of the mysteries of the universe, but can it ever solve the current problem of explaining why we cherish certain ideas as universal truths? Even if somehow such questions could be brought within the realm of science, doesn't it take just as much faith to believe science will provide answers to all of our questions as it does to believe in an omnipresent God? Are we merely creating a post-modern omniscient deity—science, whose priests wear lab coats—in place of the more traditional God?

CHAPTER SEVEN

WHAT MIGHT A SOURCE OF THE HUMAN RIGHTS URGE LOOK LIKE?

"And they said, Go to, let us build us a city and a tower,
whose top may reach unto heaven; and let us make us a name,
lest we be scattered abroad upon the face of the whole earth."

—GENESIS 11 v. 4[1]

So far, I have been building a case that we have a choice to either embrace a world of relative moral values and the chaos and depravity it logically entails, or embrace the existence of universal human rights and simultaneously the existence of absolute truth. Thinking we are not limited to this choice is a delusion.

If there are universal truths about human nature and rights, these truths must exist independent of ourselves and of the society in which we live. Where do these truths come from? In this chapter I propose a potential source of universal moral truth and the human rights urge: the Christian God.

Universal human rights are predicated upon the treatment of each person as an individual whose life is precious and sacred—a belief that all persons are inherently, equally valuable. Further, human rights are not to be selectively applied; even those considered our enemies deserve to have their fundamental human rights respected.

Any candidate for the source of the human rights urge must embody these two concepts. Additionally, a prospective source of the human rights urge must not itself have a source. It must, in fact, be the primary and first source.

If we discovered a source of the human rights urge, but then had to look for a source of this source, and so on and so on, we would end up in absurdity. If there is to be a source of the human rights urge, it must be a first source that does not itself have a source. Additionally, the source must not vary over time.

The source of absolute moral truths must reflect these truths. And it must be absolute and unchanging or immutable. If the source of absolute truth changed over time, we would be left with the same problems that a relative theory of truth brings. It would be possible for the crimes of Hitler's regime to be morally wrong when judged by the absolute truths at a point in time X, and not wrong at point in time Y because the source of absolute moral truth had changed from time X to time Y.

Utilitarian moral principles dictate that the course of action to be taken is the course that results in the best outcome for the greatest number of people. The human rights urge does not mesh with utilitarianism because the application of such principles would result in the abandonment of some individuals and groups.

For example, using utilitarian principles, it can be argued that certain problems are due to over-population. Therefore, protecting every life in an over-populated area is not in the best interest of the greatest number of people. Further, if resources such as food or medicine were scarce, these items would be rationed according to criteria whereby those who were judged to be in the best position to benefit society would be favored. Such thinking is in total opposition to the human rights urge.

The concepts of the sacredness of individual life and the application of fundamental rights to all humanity, even one's enemies, are deeply imbedded in Christianity. No other system of belief explains the persistence of the human desire to protect and enforce the rights of others who are totally unconnected with us.

In the parable of the lost sheep, Jesus articulated the Christian ideal that each individual is important and should not be sacrificed to the collective. Jesus explained God's love for every human by giving the example of a shepherd who has 100 sheep. One of the sheep gets lost. When the shepherd discovers he is missing one of his sheep, he leaves the other 99 sheep and goes to find the one missing sheep.[2]

The human rights urge demands that the protection of the fundamental rights of others be pursued regardless of cost. It is obscene to put a price on human life. The moral truth that every person is valuable and sacred, possessing certain fundamental rights worthy of protection, is reflected in Christianity. No other belief system so privileges the sacredness of individual life.

Another ideal of modern human rights theory is the protection of the rights of everyone, no matter who they are, even if they are more usually our enemies. Jesus illustrated this principle when He told the parable or story of the Good Samaritan.

This story of altruism is a perfect example of the elevation of individual rights over cultural and ethnic enmity and personal cost. The Samaritans and the Jews were traditional enemies as a result of centuries of religious strife over the proper location to worship God. The Samaritan man in the story overcame the prejudices he would inevitably have acquired as he grew up to help the Jewish man who lay bleeding on the road to Jericho. He did not count the personal cost, either in terms of the money he spent to care for the injured man or the safety risk he took to stop and help the man on a dangerous thoroughfare. There was no personal gain for the Samaritan. He did not even receive the satisfaction to be commended or rewarded for his efforts, either from society at large or the injured man.[3]

Certainly, Jesus recognized and eloquently articulated the existence of absolute moral truths, but was He merely recognizing certain preexisting moral truths?

However, Jesus did more than merely repeat the Golden Rule of doing to others what you would like them to do to you.[4] He universalized this concept.

He confronted the prejudices of His contemporary Jewish audience and made it clear that the Golden Rule meant to not just treat fellow Jews according to the Golden Rule, but Samaritans and Romans also. He admonished His Jewish audience to love their enemies as themselves. This was revolutionary and remains so to this day.

However, we do not have to look to the parables of Jesus to see how

Christianity explains the human rights urge. The central theme of Christianity embodies the truth that every human life is sacred and must be saved at any cost, even at the greatest cost.

Christianity presents the story of an all-powerful God sending his Son to die for humanity, so each human could have an opportunity to live eternally. According to Christianity, Jesus Christ was the living embodiment of God in human form. God is far greater than all of His creation, including His masterpiece: mankind.

The price of the suffering and death of Jesus, for each and every member of the human race, was worth it for God. It did not matter that most of mankind was ignorant of or hated Him, or that in a very real sense, mankind made itself an enemy of God. God sacrificed Himself for each person, many of whom would never love Him in return or even acknowledge Him—many of whom would openly oppose Him.

When we desire to help the helpless and give of ourselves to makes the lives of others better, we are mirroring God. The human rights urge is a pale shadow of the longing of God for humanity. When we truly and unselfishly help those in need, we are reflecting God.

The source of the human rights urge must be unchanging. Christianity tells us the Christian God is unchanging, eternal, and the source of all truth. So Christianity provides a source of moral truth that meets the criteria that it always remains the same.

Moreover, Christianity best articulates human rights and its underlying assumptions. Christianity values the individual as a sacred being whose existence is not to be outweighed by the needs of the collective. In addition, Christianity urges its adherents to love their enemies.

The source of the human rights urge must be absolute and immutable. Christianity presents immutable universal moral truths that find their wellspring in an immutable, eternal God. Consequently, if you want a source of the absolute values enumerated in human rights theory, Christianity deserves—at a minimum—very serious consideration.

The skeptic will most likely object that belief in God is inherently ridiculous and intellectually untenable. But, as we have seen, the skeptic's rejection of God is (more often than not) tied to an *a priori* rejection of the transcendent. As I have argued, if we wish to cling to the existence of universal moral truths, we must accept that these truths are metaphysical in nature. So, the objection to the metaphysical or supernatural must be abandoned by the skeptic who embraces the existence of universal moral truths.

Has the foregoing proved Christianity is the source of the human rights urge, or even the existence of God? No, but that is, in a very fundamental sense, beside the point. To be a Christian is to believe, based on revelation. Some things have to be accepted by faith. But I'm not talking about a blind leap of faith in the dark.

Our analysis of the nature of truth showed us that certain absolute moral truths must exist. However, because these truths lie beyond the everyday, we cannot examine and break these truths down through empirical or logical analysis.

As the Wittgenstein of the *Tractatus* would express it, we can show the existence of these truths but cannot say anything about them. Because such truths transcend philosophy and science, they can only be accessed by a medium that transcends philosophy and science.

Moreover, Christianity tells us we have free will. God has provided man with a choice whether to believe in Him or not. If God's existence were logically inescapable, there would be no free will to choose whether or not to believe in Him.

But, that is not to say that God left no clues as to His existence. The point of this book has been to examine one of these clues—namely, what I call the human rights urge. When we locate the source of the human rights urge, it should provide us with information regarding how to put the human rights urge into practice. For a moment, assume for argument's sake that Christianity explains the source of the human rights urge. What happens if we try to put the human rights urge into practice without God's inspiration? Secular human rights are an attempt to create a perfect world without God.

It is an affront to man that we cannot create the perfect world for ourselves, by ourselves. However, as we saw in Chapter 3, Jean-Paul Sartre mocked the idea that man could create a world with a perfectly functioning moral core if God did not exist. If the human rights urge is

God-inspired, we must stay true to the source or we will end up horribly off-course.

The ancient biblical story of the Tower of Babel tells of mankind's attempt to build a civilization without God. In the Book of Genesis, the first book in the Bible, God commanded Noah, his sons, and their families to be fruitful and increase to inhabit the whole earth.[5] However, instead of following this direction, men decided to stay in one place and build a great city with a magnificent tower to evidence the glory of the city and its founders for all to see.[6] The result of this great project: the confusion of languages.

God, aware that human nature was corrupt and self-seeking, knew the civilization being built at Babel would not result in utopia, but in an inherently-corrupt society where the strong would prosper at the expense of the weak. Therefore, God confused the languages of mankind, causing a lack of comprehension between the builders of this city in order to prevent them from completing it. If Christianity is the source of the human rights urge, any attempt to practically implement the human rights urge that ignores Christianity is destined for failure.

THE HUMAN RIGHTS URGE IS INHERENTLY ALTRUISTIC

Some have argued that we do not have to look to the divine to discover the source of universal moral truths. They urge that these truths evolved over time through human interaction, or even that over time humans, through interaction, came to recognize the existence of universal moral truths.[7]

Humans over time found that if they helped others, others would then help them in the future when they were in need. And, so the theory goes, these interactions became embodied in universal moral truths, such as doing to others what you would like them to do to you: the Golden Rule.

But, universal human rights are not about helping others to get something in return. Such a theory would be more likely to teach humans to help those who can help you—to be nice to your friends. It would not teach you to love your enemies.

Often the human rights urge drives us to protect those we will never meet, in places we will never go. For the most part, the human rights urge is concerned with helping others in positions of weakness who are not likely ever to be able to protect us in return.

It makes little sense to explain the urge to human rights as a global cooperation game we play because we would like others to stand up for our rights if we are someday in the position of the oppressed. We stand up for human rights because they are intrinsically worth defending, not because we look to get something from our effort. Indeed, attempting to protect the human rights of others is often an anathema to self-interest.

Evolutionary theory presents us with natural selection—the thesis that stronger and fitter creatures will survive and pass their traits on to the next generation at the expense of their weaker fellow creatures. The elimination of weaker members of society fits much easier with the theory of evolution than the assertion that an altruistic human rights urge, to help the feeble for no return, evolved over time. Indeed, the desire to respect the rights of one's enemies might significantly hamper the development of a society and its ability to defend itself from its foes.

THE POLICEMAN IN THE SKY?

Another objection raised against the contention that the source of absolute moral truth is found in Christianity is the objection that God is a human creation. Certain thinkers have postulated that God is a human creation, necessary for primitive humans to invent in order to exhort their fellows to follow certain moral and societal rules (or else, an all-powerful God would punish them).

Then, those who invented God naturally became His spokespersons, conveniently tailoring God's rules to suit their purposes. So, this theory goes, the classes of priests, or those who mediated between God and humans, grabbed power for themselves by using the threat of the wrath of God to force society to follow their rules.

Thinkers such as Voltaire, who have expressed this theory, contended that if God did not exist it would be necessary to invent Him.[8] I believe they were right, but not for the reasons they probably thought.

Modern philosophers have metaphorically killed God, but they have not succeeded in establishing a satisfactory basis for the moral sense we all, at some level, take for granted. So this slogan should be revised as follows to work in the post-modern, post-God world that many of us have decided we live in:

"If God is dead, and we wish to defend the existence of universal norms of human conduct such as those enshrined in the Universal Declaration of Human Rights, we need to resurrect Him."

Otherwise, we are damned to struggle through a world without moral absolutes in which everything is permissible, and we have no right to condemn even the most heinous of atrocities.

CHAPTER EIGHT

ON HEDONISM

"The right to swing my fist ends where the other man's nose begins."

—OLIVER WENDELL HOLMES[1]

I have argued against the theory that truth is relative or contingent. If you have followed and agree with the progression of my argument, you will accept that if truth is relative, even the vilest crimes against humanity cannot be condemned, and the endurance of principles of truth and freedom is far from guaranteed.

Moreover, you will also hopefully realize a relative theory of truth is not possible if there are no absolute truths. So why, if the theory that truth is relative is so unpalatable, does it predominate in our post-modern world today?

One obvious reason is many are ignorant of the problems that come with adherence to a relative theory of truth—hence, the purpose of this book. However, there are those aware of these issues who still fervently deny the existence of absolute truth. For example, Jean-Paul Sartre and Richard Rorty. How do such persons determine that the benefits of a relative theory of truth outweigh its many problems?

I previously suggested one reason: the embrace of absolute truth leads naturally to speculation about the existence of a supernatural or an omniscient deity who is the source of absolute moral standards. However, I think we must dig a little deeper.

The reason many are loathe to acknowledge the possibility of absolute truth is not simply because they do not wish to accept the possibility of the existence of an all-powerful, all-knowing deity. It is because they do not want to accept the consequences that follow from the existence of an all-powerful, all-knowing deity as the source of absolute moral truth.

If God is the source of moral absolutes and there are actions that are right and wrong, not everything we do is permissible. This is the heart of the appeal of relative truth, the fact that if there are no absolute moral truths, we can do what we want without condemnation. No one can tell us what to do.

This is the appealing counterpart to the problem that we cannot condemn even history's most horrible crimes if there are no absolute moral truths. If truth is relative, no one can condemn how you act, or fail to act.

As Sartre paraphrased Dostoevsky, "If God did not exist, everything would be permitted."[2] This is an enticing concept if one only applies it to oneself, and not to everyone else.

Each of us would like the ability to do what we want to do, when we want to do it, without incurring the moral approbation of others. We, however, tend to conveniently forget this also gives others the right to do whatever they want.

The application of the dictum *everything is permissible*, to oneself and the pursuit of one's own pleasure without restraint, is hedonism. Hedonism is the complete opposite of Immanuel Kant's categorical imperative[3] and the biblical admonition to treat others in the same way you would like to be treated.

We all know that if everyone could do whatever he or she wanted, the world would be a terrible place because of the trouble that would inevitably ensue. If my desire to do something opposes your desire to do something else, we will come into conflict. As the saying attributed to the American jurist Oliver Wendell Holmes goes: "The right to swing my fist ends where the other man's nose begins."[4]

If the freedom to do as we please is extended to everyone, we lose our freedom. Inevitably, our desire will clash with the desires of others. In the event of such conflict, the strongest individual could impose his or her wishes on those weaker than him or her. So, if we are the weaker party whose wishes have come into conflict with the desires of a stronger party, we will lose out. Everything is permissible, but not everything is possible without power.

Thomas Hobbes wrote about the horrors of a world where everyone had the freedom to do as they wished. The strong would victimize the weak, and violent chaos would be the order of the day. In such a world, life would be "nasty, brutish and short."[5] Hobbes's solution to this problem was that we should surrender some of our freedom and agree to be governed by a powerful sovereign who would protect the rights of individuals and maintain law and order. Hobbes maintained that because uninhibited freedom would lead to chaos, it must be curtailed by the surrender of some freedom to the state.

Embracing hedonism is shortsighted; however, at the same time, it is very enticing. We have seen that its appeal lies in the fact that it falsely promises absolute freedom to act. Why are we so blind to the other side of the equation—the ability of others to do what they want to us?

I think that the answer can be found in the shift to anthropocentrism[6] and narcissism that has occurred in post-modern society. By anthropocentrism and narcissism I refer to the post-modern obsession with self.

We have moved from a worldview where an omniscient, omnipotent God was the center of the universe and the source of all truth to a world where each of us is the center of the universe and truth is dependent upon us. We are told that we should do what makes us happy and that self-gratification is not a bad thing.

The focus on self is shown by the reverence accorded to individual, subjective beliefs even if these beliefs do not make any attempt to correlate with ultimate reality. (I will spend more time on this subject and provide specific examples in the next chapter.) Even the idea explored briefly in Chapter 7, that we humans invented God, betrays an overbearing emphasis on self.

The narcissistic worldview focuses on self and what is good for me. Since hedonism is about pursuing that which brings one pleasure, it fits well with the post-modern zeitgeist. So a theory that truth is relative to what we, as individuals, believe fits well with us because allied with selective self-induced narcissistic blindness, it justifies hedonism.

The narcissism prevalent in society is reflected in post-modern philosophical thought. The move from Plato's objective Forms to Wittgenstein's subjective Forms of Life resonates with our narcissistic tendencies. Wittgenstein's later philosophy is anthropocentric[7]— man has become the central figure.

Traditionally, philosophers like Plato envisioned man as attempting to latch on to the ultimate truths of the universe. The truth was out there somewhere to be discovered. Wittgenstein and others rejected this model, and instead proclaimed that truth was in us; we create it as we go along. So, man has gone from a relatively insignificant being, trying to grapple with the overwhelming weight of objective reality, to the subjective master of his own reality.

Given our obsession with self, it is hardly surprising we think it is fine for us to live in a world with malleable moral markers, as long as we get our own way without being bullied by others into accepting their way of doing things. We want others to respect moral boundaries that we want to be free to ignore when it suits.

Unfortunately, if we pause for a moment to consider, we know the world does not work like this. But the narcissism that permeates post-modern culture has not dragged, but lulled us here.

So one of the biggest reasons for the post-modern obsession with relative truth, that it justifies hedonism, also turns out to be problematic. In a world of relative truth, hedonism is only available to a select few with the means to pursue their desires.

But, even the powerful may, more often than not, find their wishes thwarted. We allow the wool to be pulled over our eyes so easily because we are too busy looking at ourselves to clearly see what it really happening. It is ironic that philosophers like Wittgenstein and Rorty looked to community to justify our creation of private truths—tailored to our individual needs and wants.

CHAPTER NINE

THIS IS MY TRUTH - A LA CARTE BELIEF

"What is truth?"

—PONTIUS PILATE[1]

If absolute truth exists, there are potential answers to the big questions regarding the ultimate nature of reality and moral truth. This means we can be right or wrong about what exists or what is good.

So, if we have accepted the existence of absolute truth, any belief or ideas we hold can be correct or incorrect. Moreover, if we accept the existence of absolute truth and act rationally, we should want more of our ideas or beliefs to fall into the correct, rather than the incorrect column.

However, the post-modern contention that truth is relative encourages the adoption of individual subjective beliefs. If there is no ultimate absolute truth, it doesn't really matter what we hold to be true. So, why not pick and choose what seems right? We cannot lose, as we will always be right and never wrong, because if truth is relative it is impossible to be wrong. So, why not pick beliefs that work best for us and are the most interesting?

In fact, in a world where truth is relative, it is irrational to fervently believe in anything. I suppose it might be considered rational to hold certain beliefs because of the psychological benefits one derives from them (e.g., I believe X because it makes me feel nice). However, keeping to psychological terms, might this not be better labeled as insanity?

But, if truth is absolute, picking and choosing spiritual and philosophical beliefs at random to construct our own individual set of beliefs is at best foolish. If absolute truth exists, we should care whether what we believe is true. The construction of our own unique belief systems may make us feel good about ourselves, but shouldn't we be concerned that our ideas somehow relate to ultimate reality?

Anecdotal evidence of the spread of idiosyncratic beliefs can be obtained in many cases simply through conversation with those we encounter daily. Many people no longer adhere completely to the faith of their parents or grandparents, but, at the same time, do not completely reject it either. They keep the parts of the particular belief system or faith they like and ignore those parts of which they are not so fond. For example, certain members of the Roman Catholic Church have been labeled *à la carte Catholics*, as they embrace certain parts of the teachings of that church, but reject other positions the Catholic Church has taken.

Further examples of the trend towards individual subjective beliefs can be gleaned from the emergence of various forums designed to facilitate the expression of such beliefs. In the introduction to this book I mentioned the National Public Radio series *This I Believe*. Participants in this series recorded short monologues detailing their individual beliefs. Beliefs expressed by participants were highly subjective in nature and varied greatly.

The point of the series seemed to be that we can learn something from the beliefs of others—that the individual wisdom of other people has great value. No doubt. But is it wise to develop certain beliefs without worrying whether these beliefs fit with what actually is? The elevation of subjective belief and the reverence for individual beliefs encourages everyone to develop their own subjective beliefs.

I offer the following analogy of post-modern unique belief systems. It is as if I were to claim that Toronto is the capital city of Canada because I thought this to be a good idea, without caring whether my claim is true. I know Canada has a capital city and that this knowledge can be obtained by some quick research. However, I like the uniqueness of my belief. It is more important to me that my belief is personal and makes me feel good than whether it is true. My belief that Toronto is the capital of Canada also has the advantage of superficial plausibility.

Of course, we know there is a correct answer to this question: what is the capital city of Canada? We also know (and if we do not know, we can quickly determine it using an internet search engine) that Ottawa, not Toronto, is the correct response to this question. In reality no one would claim Toronto is the capital city of Canada without believing it to be a true statement (assuming, of course, that person wanted to be truthful). Even if a person had not researched the answer to the question, he or she may rely on his or her personal general knowledge to supply the correct answer.

If he or she stated that Toronto was the capital city of Canada and was told of his or her mistake, he or she would not argue that he or she still preferred his or her answer. He or she would not assert that, because Toronto is more populous than Ottawa, it would make a better capital than Ottawa. Instead, he or she would correct his or her general knowledge and try in future to remember Ottawa is the capital city of Canada.

The example above may appear ridiculous, but it points to the foolishness of clinging to subjective beliefs in the face of absolute truth. It is probably not the best idea to answer a question that demands a factual answer without first having some idea of the correct answer (unless, of course, we do not care if we appear uninformed or ignorant).

Some may even think it lazy or careless not to at least attempt to research the answer to the factual question. Similarly, if there are real answers to moral questions and questions about ultimate reality, it is odd to present random answers to such questions without caring whether the answer is correct. Of course, it is harder to answer whether a certain action is morally good than it is to answer what the capital city of Canada is, but the principle is the same.

Again we come to a contradiction that runs like a fault line through post-modern society. We want to present some issues in terms of moral relativism and others in terms of absolutes. We want to have our cake and eat it too. Is it an unwillingness to get to the bottom of certain issues for fear of what we may discover as a result of in-depth examination?

For example, when it comes to human rights, we will be hard-pressed to find a person in our society who does not profess that imprisonment without trial or murder is morally wrong. While there are social and political debates about instances of imprisonment without trial or murder, we do not debate the truth of the core concepts (e.g., that murder or imprisonment without trial is morally wrong).

Instead, we debate about facts surrounding the moral issue (e.g., that the actions in question did not constitute murder or that there was an adequate and impartial judicial procedure before incarceration). No one will say, "Yes, she murdered him in cold blood, but what is wrong with that?" or say, "They locked him up and threw away the key without caring if he was guilty, and it was the right thing to do."

If someone uttered such statements, we would consider him or her to be morally bankrupt. Conversely, with many other beliefs, we are content to accept the exponential spread of subjective *à la carte* beliefs.

SOUND-BITE BELIEFS

Another factor contributing to the proliferation of subjective idiosyncratic beliefs is the advent of the sound bite. We are used to receiving and digesting our world in small pithy chunks. We live in a society where sound bites are the normal discourse. This, of course, leads to a lot of people complaining they have been quoted out of context.

We, encouraged by the media, seize upon the most colorful or controversial statements without bothering to determine how these statements fit into the whole of what the person was trying to convey. When one watches 24-hour news channels, small summaries are provided for our convenience at the bottom of the screen even though we are supposedly paying attention to what is being said.

The sound-bite culture has infiltrated our belief systems also. We want to have a one-sentence reduction of all facts and beliefs that is easy to assimilate without too much mental strain on our part.

For the veracity of a particular news sound bite we look to the source. If we think the source is credible, we will believe the sound bite. By doing so we subcontract the task of thinking hard to others—sources we trust. But, increasingly, it appears those we think are engaged in intellectual travails on our behalf, those who are digging deep to discover truth, may, in fact, also be victims of the sound-bite culture.

We have gone down the same track regarding philosophical and religious beliefs. We do not want to have to read and agonize over obscure and difficult texts; we do not want to have to reconcile difficult and conflicting concepts; we want a smattering of beliefs written on the side of our disposable coffee cups. We can gently and quickly evaluate the belief presented in twenty words or less or the side of the mostly-recyclable container in sixty seconds or less, without breaking out of our early morning fog. If we like it, we may think about it for a couple of minutes or so until the next enticing sound bite comes our way—whether it be on television, radio, or the internet.

The result of the acceptance of the sound bite is the poverty of effort directed towards understanding ideas we encounter. On the surface, many ideas seem appealing and plausible, but may not hold up to a rigorous examination of their underlying assumptions. Rarely are ideas subject to an examination of their foundations. This has led, in part, to the holding of contradictory or even nonsensical beliefs whose true nature is only revealed after some mental effort (e.g., the fervent belief and advancement of universal human rights alongside the simultaneous rejection of the existence of absolute truth).

As I have argued, in order to discover truth it is necessary to coldly dissect and examine all of our prejudices and inherent biases to ensure we receive unbiased answers. This takes effort. It is always easier to simply accept the ideas presented to us than to question the status quo.

CHAPTER TEN

SOME THOUGHTS ON ART

"Once out of nature I shall never take
My bodily form from any natural thing,
But such a form as Grecian goldsmiths make
Of hammered gold and gold enamelling
To keep a drowsy Emperor awake;
Or set upon a golden bough to sing
To lords and ladies of Byzantium
Of what is past, or passing, or to come."

—W.B. YEATS[1]

To take a few steps from the path we have been on, let us look at how the existence or non-existence of absolute truth affects an important and cherished aspect of human endeavor—art. Whether we accept or reject the existence of absolute truth has implications for how we view art. Looking at the themes we have been examining through the prism of art and what is beautiful will, hopefully, illuminate the points made so far.

To pursue our objective, we will examine the following question: Does art provide us with truths that transcend the everyday, or is the value of art culturally contingent? In other words, are our ideas of art and beauty indoctrinated into us by the particular societies in which we grow up, or do they come from somewhere else? The answer to this first question will determine our responses to the following two questions.

First, can artists reveal meaningful truths through their chosen mediums of expression? Second, is the value of great art enduring, potentially lasting in perpetuity?

Now, let us put these issues in more concrete form. Is Michelangelo's

Sistine Chapel beautiful because we have been taught it is, or do view-
ers spontaneously declare its beauty because there are universal concepts
of beauty to which they connect this work? Can a writer such as Leo Tolstoy through his novels illuminate certain truths about the human con-
dition that are universal? Will the poetry of W.B. Yeats be admired and
valued for its artistic merits for all time?

BEAUTY IN THE EYE OF THE BEHOLDER?

Can anything be beautiful or a work of art? Vomit on a street corner?
A smashed-up car? A dead shark in a tank of formaldehyde?[2] As society has shifted increasingly towards post-modern paradigms, the concept of what is considered beautiful art has moved in a corresponding
direction.

Many ordinary and unskilled observers of the art world, in whose
number I count myself, question whether some pieces exhibited in major
galleries or awarded prestigious prizes are really works of art.[3] Is an
unmade bed a work of art?[4] Do some post-modern pieces evidence the
reductio ad absurdum of art? The evaluation of what is beautiful art has
increasingly become the domain of educated professional critics who can
discern true artistic merit where often the ordinary person cannot.

In 1984, because truth was relative, Big Brother and the Inner Party
molded it in whatever way suited their purposes. Eventually, the truth
became manipulated in so many ways and often in contradictory direc-
tions that it lost all meaning.

Winston Smith could not cling to truth because the Inner Party had
destroyed truth. Is the same thing happening to art? Are art and beauty
now what critics claim they are? Or, are there pieces of art that are intrinsically beautiful, independent of whether they receive a stamp of approval
from a professional critic?

If you were never told that Beethoven's Ninth Symphony, Shakespeare's sonnets, or Michelangelo's Sistine Chapel was beautiful, would
you think any less of them on a first encounter? I am not talking about
a deep appreciation of each of the themes or historical background of a
particular Shakespearian sonnet, or of the harmonic nuances of

Beethoven, I mean the first naked primal experience of these works. If you were to hear Beethoven for the first time, without any previous knowledge of him or his work, how would you be struck?

If there are no absolute truths, art cannot be universal. The contingent view of truth espoused by Wittgenstein in his later work would reduce the appreciation of art to a language game we are taught to play early in life. According to this theory, when we hear a piece of music like Beethoven's Ninth Symphony, we are taught to say that this is a beautiful piece of music.

Similarly, we are taught to exclaim that Shakespeare uses the English language in the most inventive and expressive way. So, if you accept this theory, our responses to what is beautiful or what is art are conditioned by, and contingent upon, societal indoctrination.

Therefore, if we accept the theory that all truth is relative, we are signing up to the fact that there is nothing intrinsically wondrous or beautiful in Beethoven's Ninth, Shakespeare's sonnets, or Michelangelo's Sistine Chapel. It follows, from an acceptance of the theory that truth is contingent upon societal indoctrination, that a society could come about in which Shakespeare's sonnets and Beethoven's symphonies are not considered beautiful works of art, but hideous grating assaults on the human senses.

Is this a consequence of belief in relative truth we are willing to accept? If there is nothing essentially beautiful in great works of art, and art gets to be beautiful upon receipt of the admiration of a qualified critic, then anything a critic labels as art is art. Instead of the Sistine Chapel, vomit on a street corner might be considered the highest form of human artistic expression.

Skeptics might argue that many people do not appreciate or like Shakespeare, Beethoven, or Michelangelo and consider other things to be more deserving of the label art. They could further point out that responses to works of art are essentially individual and subjective.

However, the fact that we perceive what is beautiful or what is art to be something others can share shows that the idea of what is beautiful or what is art cannot be totally private and subjective. Indeed, if the idea of what is beautiful were totally individual and subjective, could we even have a concept of art?

In other words, can something be beautiful or a work of art just because we say it is, or do we need at least one person to concur with our conclusion? As Wittgenstein pointed out in his Private Language Argument (discussed at the end of Chapter 3), concepts such as beauty must be public and not private in nature. Subjectivity must have an end point, or we end up in the absurd position of someone advocating the artistic merits of vomit on a street corner.

I would argue that whatever people consider beautiful or art is based on how a particular piece of music, writing, or painting initially strikes them and how they connect this first impression with their concepts of beauty and art. So, if you do not like Shakespeare, Beethoven or Michelangelo, take whatever you think to be a beautiful work of art and consider whether you would consider that thing to be beautiful if you suddenly encountered it without any previous experience or conception of it.

Would you consider this item to be beautiful no matter what cultural education or upbringing you had received? Do you accept the possibility you might not think it beautiful or even consider it horrendously ugly if your cultural experience had been different? If truth is relative, then you have no choice but to accept this proposition as true.

ILLUMINATING THE HUMAN CONDITION

What about the claim that art can provide us with fundamental truths about our world and ourselves? What does this mean? What is the nature of the truths revealed by artists? If it is relative truth, is it really useful at all?

If Tolstoy provides insight on human nature in *Anna Karenina*, are these truths contingent upon our society, or are they true for all societies and for all time? If we are willing to grant the artist license to reveal absolute truths, should we not also bestow this ability to the moral philosopher?

LOOKING TO IMMORTALITY

Is art timeless? In his poem, *Sailing to Byzantium*, W.B. Yeats sought to be transformed from decaying human flesh to a golden sculpture of a bird that would not decay. He was expressing the idea that art is eternal and his hope to leave a lasting artistic legacy long after his physical body had decomposed.

But if there are no absolute truths, is art eternal? No.

Yeats' poetry, while still appreciated for its beauty today, is not guaranteed continued appreciation in the future if truth is not absolute. If our conception of Yeats' poetry as beautiful is contingent upon how we have been indoctrinated by society, remove that indoctrination and the beauty of his poetry disappears.

So a person who did not receive the same cultural indoctrination as we did would not think the poetry beautiful and may even be appalled by it. Even if our current society values Yeats' poetry as beautiful, this might change over time as society changes.

Can the artistic expression of an Elizabethan poet and playwright remain relevant in the 21st century? Judging by the manner in which Shakespeare's appeal appears undiminished today, I would have to say yes.

But, if we believe that certain works of art are timeless, our belief is incompatible with a relative theory of truth. If we claim that the truths of art (i.e., whether a particular painting, sculpture, or musical composition is beautiful) are absolute, but cling to moral relativism, how can you justify this special pleading? Is it consistent to permit the truths of art to be absolute while condemning moral truths to relativity?

So if there are no absolute truths, we must give up the possibility of finding in art timeless truths that transcend particular historical and cultural moments. In earlier chapters, the problems of a relative theory of truth were exposed in relation to the issue of moral standards. If everything is right, nothing can be wrong.

Similarly, we can see this problem from a different angle by looking at the interaction of a relative theory of truth and art. If anything can be beautiful or a work of art, everything is beautiful—but at the same time, nothing is beautiful.

➤

CHAPTER ELEVEN

FINAL THOUGHTS

*"He, O men, is the wisest who like Socrates, knows
that his wisdom is in truth worth nothing."*

—SOCRATES[1]

I n this final chapter I would like not just to summarize what has gone before, but to also point out what might be next. This chapter is not merely a final opportunity to persuade you to accept my arguments, but also a call to action.

Much of this book has been concerned with pointing out the impossibility of the co-existence of relative truth and what I have called the human rights urge. But my point is not to belittle the urge to human rights. In fact, my goal lies in the completely opposite direction.

The desire to protect the rights of those who are oppressed is fundamental to our nature because when we fight for those who cannot protect themselves we are acting in the most authentic way. My central point is that the human rights urge is tangible and vital and that it, in turn, points us to an ultimate universal truth—the existence of moral absolutes.

Only when we marry the human rights urge with the existence of absolute truth can a true picture of human rights emerge. We have established that if we are to accept the human rights urge, we must simultaneously accept the existence of absolute moral truths. Once we have done this, we must then acknowledge that the source of absolute moral truth must be independent of our society and ourselves.

Next, we address the fact that the source of absolute moral standards must be unchanging. When we look for a source of the human rights urge, this source must reflect, or rather the human rights urge must reflect, that source. I have argued that Christianity meets these criteria.

The implications of this line of argument for non-Christians are plain enough. That is to say that non-Christians owe it to themselves to explore whether they truly embrace the human rights urge. If they do, they should then look for a source of the universal truths that underlie the human rights urge. If they approach this matter without bias, they should carefully evaluate Christianity as a strong possibility for the source of the human rights urge.

But what does this mean for Christians? I believe that authentic Christianity compels its adherents to embrace the urge to help others as an outpouring of their faith. Christians are the true inheritors of the admonition to protect the rights of the oppressed and the hurting. Christians must embrace Jesus' command to treat every human life as special and sacred, even the lives of their enemies.

Throughout this book, I have contended that by focusing on the physical needs and suffering of humanity while ignoring the transcendent inspiration of the human rights urge, we run down blind alleys such as moral relativism. Conversely, Christians must not become so enamored by the transcendent that they forget about the temporal.

Often, contemporary Christians are put to shame by non-Christians who practically implement the human rights urge while Christians watch from the sidelines. Christians should meditate on the truths embodied in the parable of the Good Samaritan to consider how they can help bind up the wounds of this world, even if the wounded are not those Christians are most used to or comfortable associating with.

POST-MODERN DOUBLE-THINKING

As I stated in the introduction to this final chapter, you will not find an exhaustive summary of the arguments put forward in this book here. So, instead, here is an example from one of the twentieth century's most insightful and prescient writers to sum it all up.

I have argued strongly that the world George Orwell portrays in *1984* could not come about because of the existence of absolute truth. But, there are many ideas raised by Orwell that do ring true in our post-modern society. Chief among these is *doublethink. Doublethink* was an ability developed by *Inner Party* members to simultaneously intellectually accept two contradictory beliefs.

Winston Smith worked for the Ministry of Truth where he was tasked with falsifying the past. He daily received instructions to amend newspaper archives to accord with the *Inner Party's* needs. He constantly rewrote the past, sometimes changing the same event multiple times.

Doublethink required him to accept the truth of statements and proclamations of the *Inner Party* while at the same time, in order to properly pursue his vocation, remaining fully-conscious that the statements of the *Inner Party* were riddled with so many untruths that no one could ever reconstruct the truth of anything. Winston was forced to believe there was no puppet master while he, though not the puppet master, was at least partly involved in pulling some of the strings.

The key to *doublethink* is that one must ignore truth when it is convenient to do so, even though this is logically untenable. Logic, through the law of the excluded middle, tells us that proposition A and its direct contradiction—proposition B—cannot both be true at the same time.

To illustrate, the statements "The car is red." and "The car is blue." cannot be true of the same car, at the same time (assuming the car is only one color). To argue both statements are true of the same car at the same time would be illogical because it violates a fundamental law of logic.

We engage in *doublethink* when we concurrently give intellectual assent to moral relativism and universal human rights because, like Winston in *1984*, we focus on the puppet show and pretend we don't see the strings. That is to say, moral relativism asserts that the puppet show is the only game in town.

However, when we carefully consider concepts like freedom, equality, and justice, embodied and protected by international human rights law standards, we receive a clue that these concepts must be inspired by something greater than the everyday. To deny there is nothing more than the puppet show after gaining this metaphysical inkling is to consciously choose to remain unconscious.

My hope is that reading this book will inspire you to stop ignoring the strings and acknowledge that the puppet show is not all that there is. But, that is only the first part. The next step is to make an unbiased, good-faith attempt to discover where the strings lead. However, even if we do not agree on the source of universal absolute truth, hopefully after finishing this book, you will at least acknowledge that it doesn't matter what you believe—if it's not true.

NOTES

CHAPTER 1

1. Plato, "Apology." Translated by Benjamin Jowett. In *The Trial and Death of Socrates: Four Dialogues*, 41. New York: Barnes & Noble, 2004.

2. *See, for example,* Lewis, C.S., *Mere Christianity*. New York: Walker & Company, 1987.

3. "This I Believe | A Public Dialogue about Belief – One Essay at a Time." Accessed July 26, 2011. http://thisibelieve.org.

4. Hobbes, Thomas. *Leviathan*. London: Penguin Books, 1985. 186.

CHAPTER 2

1. Whitehead, Alfred North. Edited by David Ray Griffin and Donald W. Sherburne. *Process and Reality: an Essay in Cosmology*. New York: Free Press, 1978. 39.

2. Ibid.

3. Plato, Translated by Robin Waterfield. *Republic*. New York: Oxford UP, 1994. 240–45.

4. *The Cambridge Dictionary of Philosophy*. Edited by Robert Audi. Cambridge : Cambridge University Press, 1995. 812-13.

5. Ibid.

6. Hume, David. *Enquiries: Concerning Human Understanding and Concerning the Principles of Morals*. Oxford: Oxford University Press, 1992. 152.

7. Kant, Immanuel. Translated by J.M.D. Meiklejohn. *Critique of Pure Reason*. New York: Barnes & Noble, 2004. xxxviii, note 13.

8. Hume, David. *A Treatise of Human Nature*. Oxford: Clarendon, 1967. 269.

9. *See, for example,* Ayer, A.J. *Language, Truth, and Logic*. New York: Dover Publications, 1952.

10. Heidegger, Martin. Translated by John Macquarrie and Edward Robinson. *Being and Time*. New York: HarperPerennial, 2008.

11. Wittgenstein, Ludwig. "Tractatus Logico Philosophicus." In *Major Works*, 82. New York: HarperPerennial, 2009.

12. Wittgenstein, Ludwig. Translated by G. E. M. Anscombe, P. M. S. Hacker, and Joachim Schulte. *Philosophische Untersuchungen - Philosophical Investigations*. Chichester, West Sussex, UK: Wiley-Blackwell, 2009. 99, Investigation #261.

13. Ibid, 15, Investigation #23.

14. Ibid, 125, Investigation #384.

15. Ibid, 106, Investigation #293.

CHAPTER 3

1. Orwell, George. *Nineteen Eighty-four*. London: Penguin, 1990. 280.

2. Sartre, Jean-Paul. Transalated by Philip Mairet. *Existentialism and Humanism*. London: Methuen, 1952. 33–34.

3. Orwell, *Nineteen Eighty-four*, 55.

4. Ibid, 18.

5. Rorty, Richard. *Contingency, Irony, and Solidarity*. Cambridge: Cambridge University Press, 1989. 173.

6. Ibid, 175–76.

7. Wittgenstein, *Philosophische Untersuchungen - Philosophical Investigations*, 106–7, Investigation #293.

CHAPTER 4

1. "The Universal Declaration of Human Rights." United Nations. Accessed July 26, 2011. http://www.un.org/en/documents/udhr/.

2. *See* Janis, Mark. "Individuals as Subjects of International Law." *Cornell International Law Journal* 17 (1984): 61.

3. *See* Halberstam, Malvina. "Belgium's Universal Jurisdiction Law: Vindication Of International Justice Or Pursuit Of Politics?" *Cardozo Law Review* 25 (2003): 247.

4. "The Avalon Project : Judgment of the International Military Tribunal for the Trial of German Major War Criminals." In *Avalon Project - Documents in Law, History and Diplomacy*. Accessed July 26, 2011. http://avalon.law.yale.edu/imt/judgen.asp.

5. *See* May, Richard, and Marieke Wierda. "Trends in International

Criminal Evidence: Nuremberg, Tokyo, The Hague, and Arusha." *Columbia Journal of Transnational Law* 37 (1999): 725.

6. *See* "ICC – About the Court." International Criminal Court. Accessed July 26, 2011. www.icc-cpi.int/Menus/ICC/About+the+Court/.

7. "The Universal Declaration of Human Rights." http://www.un.org/en/documents/udhr/

8. Orwell, *Nineteen Eighty-four*, 18.

9. Solzhenitsyn, Alexander. Translated by Thomas P. Whitney. *Gulag Archipelago 1918–1956*. Glasgow: William Collins, 1974.

10. *See, for example, The Insider*. Directed by Michael Mann. Performed by Russell Crowe, Al Pacino, and Christopher Plummer. Burbank: Walt Disney Video, 2000. DVD.

CHAPTER 5

1. Lincoln, Abraham. "A House Divided." Speech, Illinois Republican Party's Nomination Acceptance as United States Senator, Illinois Statehouse, Springfield, June 16 1858.

2. *See* Overbye, Dennis. "Wisdom in a Cleric's Garb; Why Not a Lab Coat Too?" *New York Times* (New York), June 1, 2009, D2 sec.

CHAPTER 6

1. Attributed to Voltaire.

2. *See* Kant, *Critique of Pure Reason*, 13.

3. Wittgenstein, "Tractatus Logico Philosophicus," 82.

4. Ibid. 81.

5. *See* Pears, David. *Wittgenstein*. London: Fontana, 1971. 88.

CHAPTER 7

1. Genesis. In *King James Version*, Public Domain. 11:4-9.

2. Luke. 15:1–7.

3. Luke. 10:29–37.

4. Matthew. 7:12.

5. Genesis. 9:1.

6. Genesis. 11.

7. *See* Wright, Robert. "A Grand Bargain Over Evolution," *New York Times* (New York), August 23, 2009, WK9 sec.

8. Attributed to Voltaire.

CHAPTER 8

1. Attributed to Justice Oliver Wendell Holmes, Jr.
2. Sartre, *Existentialism and Humanism*, 33-34.
3. *See* Kant, Immanuel. *Grounding for the Metaphysics of Morals*. Translated by James W. Ellington. Indianapolis: Hackett Pub. 1981.
4. Attributed to Justice Oliver Wendell Holmes. Jr.
5. Hobbes, *Leviathan*, 186.
6. See the use of this term in Pears, *Wittgenstein*, 31-41.
7. Ibid.

CHAPTER 9

1. John. In *King James Version*, Public Domain. 18:38.

CHAPTER 10

1. Yeats, W. B. "Sailing to Byzantium." In *The Collected Poems of W.B. Yeats*, 217-18. London: Macmillan, 1952.
2. Hirst, Damien. *The Physical Impossibility of Death in the Mind of Someone Living*. Artchive, 1991. Accessed July 26, 2011. http://www.artchive.com/artchive/H/hirst.html.
3. *See* Gibbons, Fiachra. "Scandal Sheets Envelop Turner Prize." The Guardian. October 20, 1999. Accessed July 26, 2011. http://www.guardian.co.uk/uk/1999/oct/20/fiachragibbons.
4. Emin, Tracey. "My Bed." Artnet. 1998. Accessed July, 26, 2011. http://www.artnet.com/artwork/424484025/tracey-emin-my-bed.html.

CHAPTER 11

1. Plato, "Apology." 26.